His Bitterness
Tore at Her Heart!

Alex wanted to go to Marcos, to hold him and comfort him. Only another artist, to whom music meant life, could understand the awesome, soul-destroying loss Marcos Rivera had suffered. It had little to do with the loss of his career. It was the terrible inability to satisfy needs and longings in the heart and soul that demanded expression.

What she felt must have shown in her face, for suddenly he flew at her, his face contorted into a savage mask of hatred. "Get out!" he snarled. "I don't need you . . . your pity. Not from a woman!"

_____

DIANA DIXON

has visited every state in the continental U.S., Europe and Mexico. Every summer, she retreats to her mountain cabin in Utah to write. Presently residing in Terre Haute, Indiana, Ms. Dixon reveals that "eighteen years of happy marriage, two terrific children and a husband who gets more handsome with the passing years" makes her a great believer in romance.

Dear Reader,

Silhouette Special Editions are an exciting new line of contemporary romances from Silhouette Books. Special Editions are written specifically for our readers who want a story with heightened romantic tension.

Special Editions have all the elements you've enjoyed in Silhouette Romances and *more*. These stories concentrate on romance in a longer, more realistic and sophisticated way, and they feature greater sensual detail.

I hope you enjoy this book and all the wonderful romances from Silhouette. We welcome any suggestions or comments and invite you to write to us at the address below.

Karen Solem
Editor-in-Chief
Silhouette Books
P.O. Box 769
New York, N. Y. 10019

DIANA DIXON
Mexican Rhapsody

Silhouette Special Edition
Published by Silhouette Books New York
America's Publisher of Contemporary Romance

Other Silhouette Books by Diana Dixon

Return Engagement

SILHOUETTE BOOKS, a Simon & Schuster Division of
GULF & WESTERN CORPORATION
1230 Avenue of the Americas, New York, N.Y. 10020

ISBN: 0-671-53503-X

First Silhouette Books printing February, 1982

10 9 8 7 6 5 4 3 2 1

Map by Tony Ferrara

America's Publisher of Contemporary Romance

Printed in the U.S.A.

Mexican
Rhapsody

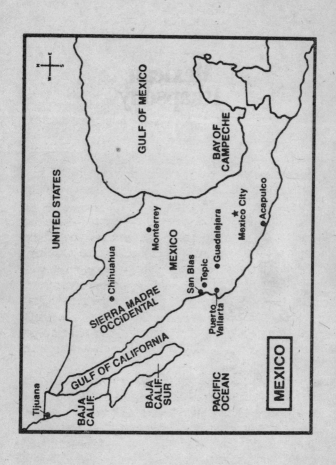

Chapter One

*A*lex leaned her head against the hard back of the leather easy chair and watched her father as he paced the floor of the dressing room with nervous energy. He was always like this just before a concert, his white tie and tails immaculate but his graying hair ruffled by his restless fingers—and pacing, always pacing. Many was the time that she envied him his seemingly endless vitality. They had traveled all night and not arrived in Boston until the early hours of the morning, but still he showed no sign of fatigue from the long flight from London and a day spent in rehearsal.

Methodically Alex pleated the soft fabric of her black crêpe gown and then smoothed the material out and down over her knees. It was these final moments of waiting that she hated most of all. This was when tension tightened the muscles through her shoulders and down the back of her neck and brought a frown to her usually serene face. Fortunately, she knew that once onstage and seated at the piano, her nervousness would be dispelled.

Absently she looked around the impersonal dressing room. They were all alike, these windowless basement rooms. This one could just as well be in Tokyo, Sydney, Manila. All the same. Sometimes she felt that half her life had been spent like this—restlessly sitting, watching her father, impatiently waiting for the stage manager's call.

With a sigh she picked up the newspaper that lay on the table beside her and turned to the arts section. As she expected, photos of her father and herself stared somberly at her from the printed page. The cutline underneath was brief: *Alexandra and Nikolas Stephanos in duo-recital at Symphony Hall.* The story that accompanied the picture was the usual press release, a listing of their credits followed by a description of the program they would perform in three successive concerts.

Alex grimaced at the artistically posed photos. The touched-up picture of her father made him look ten years younger than his fifty-six years, she mused wryly, while her own added ten years to her age. They looked more like husband and wife or brother and sister than father and daughter.

She nearly tossed the paper aside when a familiar name caught her attention: Marcos Rivera. The article was short, just the notice that the world-renowned pianist had been released from the hospital in Mexico City and that as yet the doctors refused to comment on the success of the operation.

Alex frowned and reread the story. What operation? She had been out of the country for so long that she had lost all touch with news. She hadn't even known that he had been ill. A vivid picture of him flashed to her mind, and somehow she could not imagine the strong, dynamic Marcos Rivera anything but perfectly fit.

She had only seen him play once, when she was sixteen, a music student in London, and Pieter van Loos, her father's friend and manager, had taken her to the concert at Albert Hall. Rivera had played a Rachmaninoff program, and she had come away both elated and depressed. He was a true genius, and his performance had been electrifying, but she sadly doubted that she would ever play with even half his combination of technique and passion.

Afterward Pieter had taken her to a reception and introduced her to the young virtuoso —and she had never forgotten the experience. Brief though the encounter had been, she had been awestruck by the sheer magnetism that emanated from the man, and when he smiled, she realized that a great deal of his success with mass audiences was due as much to his charisma as to his playing.

From then on, she had become his devoted fan. She had bought every record he ever made, followed his career in the papers and trade journals . . .

"Alex!"

Alex jumped and nearly dropped the paper. Her father had stopped his pacing and stood before her. His irritated frown told her he had been trying—obviously with no success—to get her attention.

"I think I want to change the encore. Schubert does not feel right tonight. We will do the Shostakovich prelude!"

Such changes were not uncommon with Nikolas. His artistic sensibilities picked up vibrations from an audience that escaped Alex. She knew that tonight he sensed excitement in the air, and the Schubert would be too tame for him. After all, this was their first concert in the United States after nearly six months' absence.

Before Alex could reply—although no reply was really expected or sought—the door was flung open and an elderly man in full formal dress sailed majestically into the room.

"Pieter!" Alex cried and jumped to her feet to greet the unexpected arrival.

"Alexandra! My dear child!" Pieter van Loos beamed. "You grow lovelier each time I see you! But so thin! Are you starving her, Nikolas?"

"Pieter!" A rare smile broke over the violinist's face as he first shook the extended hand and then embraced the older man.

Van Loos's short, stocky frame quivered

with pleasure as he returned the embrace of his onetime protégé.

"We did not think to see you tonight, Pieter," Nikolas continued as he released his hold. "Your secretary told us you were out of the country, and she did not seem to know where you were or when you would return."

"For the rest of the world, I gave her instructions to be discreet." He shrugged with an airy wave of the hand. "But for you, no! And did you think I would miss your return? Never!"

Turning to Alex, he took both her hands in his own pudgy, beautifully manicured ones and raised each to his lips as he smiled into her warm brown eyes. "Six months! Six months since I have seen my darling! But I read the notices. They loved you—everywhere! As, of course, I knew they would." His pigeon chest puffed with pride, and he beamed happily at Alex, his eyes crinkling up at the corners until they nearly disappeared into his face.

Impulsively Alex hugged him and pressed a kiss on his soft, florid cheek. He was such a dear, much more a father to her actually than her own.

A quick knock on the door interrupted the reunion. "Ten minutes, Mr. Stephanos!"

"I will leave you now," van Loos said, reluctantly releasing Alex. "But tonight after the performance, you will join me for supper, *ja*? I have invited many of your friends in to welcome you back. And you will eat, Alexandra. We must begin to put some meat on your bones, or the sea breeze will carry you away!"

His departure was as abrupt as his arrival, and with no time to waste, Alex took one last glance in the mirror, smoothing the already neat chestnut hair over her ears and patting the tight chignon at the nape of her neck. She caught sight of her father's reflection in the mirror and winced.

"Your hair, Nikolas! Here, use my comb."

Nikolas Stephanos ran the comb carelessly through his hair, giving it a degree of order, and then lovingly picked up his violin from the open case. Not even looking to see if Alex followed, he led the way into the corridor and across to the circular stairs that led to the stage above.

In the wings they waited silently together. The massive curtain was drawn and the stage was bare except for the huge concert grand piano. From what Alex could see of the audience through the small slit in the side of the curtain, the house was packed, and a low, expectant murmur drifted to where they stood.

At last the houselights began to dim and a hush settled over the audience as the lights came up on the stage. Nervously Alex reached out for her father's hand, and together they walked to the center of the stage, acknowledging with a bow and a curtsy the applause that greeted them. Alex caught the smile of pleasure and gleam of satisfaction that came into Nikolas's eyes. Never was he happier than at a moment like this, when an evening of music lay ahead of him and the audience was excited and expectant. Then the smile faded into concentration as Alex took her place at the piano and he stood in the curve, tucked the violin comfortably under his chin, and raised his bow. Alex's hands were poised over the keys, awaiting his signal. The concert was about to begin.

Two hours later, Alex took her hands from the keys and drew a deep breath before beginning the *gigue* that was the final movement of the Bach suite. She met her father's eye, caught his nod, and brought her hands down firmly. She knew that she had probably never played better than this evening. Nikolas had been in magnificent form, and his brilliance lifted Alex to new heights as he coaxed, caressed, demanded response from his instrument—the same way a skilled lover would manipulate a woman, Alex had often thought. And Alex joined him with renewed energy.

Nikolas was a cold man, reserving all his emotion for his audience and his playing, and he had been uninterested in eliciting love or even affection from his daughter, but his very genius demanded her utmost respect and admiration. And tonight she gave him both in abundance.

In absolute unity and harmony they

reached the culminating crescendo, and Alex played with a sureness and power that seemed impossible from her slight frame. The final notes drifted into silence in the packed auditorium. Then followed the breathless quiet—the greatest praise of all—and finally the applause. The huge concert hall rang with the enthusiastic ovation. Almost as a body the audience rose to its feet.

Again and again Alex and Nikolas bowed. And then Nikolas—in what was for Alex an unprecedented and never-to-be-forgotten gesture—took her hand and raised it to his lips. Alex's eyes blurred with tears as just for a moment she saw on his face a respect and pride he had never shown her before. Humbly she swept him a deep curtsy as the crowd went wild. This night, this concert, would live for years to come in the memories of those who had been privileged to see it.

"Nearly noon, Miss Alex," the housekeeper said cheerfully, then smiled as the girl groaned and buried her head deeper in the covers. "You want I should let you sleep some more?"

"No, Ruthy," Alex mumbled, but she showed no signs of reviving.

"You want I should bring your coffee in here?" the older woman persisted.

"No, I'll get up. Just give me a few minutes." Still no signs of life in the recumbent form.

"That must have been some party last night." Ruth Frazer grinned as she began picking up the clothes that Alex had discarded carelessly in the early hours of the morning. They formed a trail from the door to the bed and then on to the bathroom. "I've never known Mr. Nikolas to sleep so long. You both must have been worn out."

That piece of information brought Alex out of her semiconscious state. "Nikolas isn't up yet?" she asked in surprise. "I thought he was meeting Pieter at eleven."

"Mr. van Loos called, but when I told him Mr. Nikolas was still asleep, he said both of you could come in later this afternoon. About three."

Sighing, Alex pulled herself to a sitting position and pushed back the heavy waves of hair that fell in her face. Released at night from its usual tight bun, her hair seemed to take on a life of its own.

"You know, Miss Alex"—Ruthy laughed— "you look about twelve years old in that pink nightie with your hair all over your face."

Alex grimaced and pulled down the sleeves of her no-nonsense cotton nightgown. She did indeed look like a teenager with the heavy makeup removed from her eyes and her face all shiny from the cold cream. But not even the thick cotton could completely erase the full, mature curves of her breasts.

"How did you manage to keep busy while we were gone?" she asked with genuine interest. Ruth Frazer had served Alex and her father for many years. In fact, she had been with the family since Alex was born, when Nikolas Stephanos, an aspiring violinist, had been simply Nicholas Stephens, son of immigrant Greek parents who had settled in Boston and Americanized their name. It had been Pieter van Loos, the brilliant Dutch impresario, who had recognized the young Nicholas's potential, changed his name back to the Greek, and launched his career. It had been Pieter also who had acknowledged Alex's own brilliance and urged Nikolas to perform in duo-recital with his daughter on the concert circuit. That had been four years before. Ruthy, who had raised Alex after her mother's death when the child was three, now stayed in Boston and kept the apartment ready for their sporadic visits.

"I've been taking cooking classes," Ruthy replied in answer to the question.

"Cooking classes!"

"Yep. You know, the fancy kind. You wait till you taste the seafood crêpe I've whipped up for your lunch today! You're too thin, Alex! I hope you and Mr. Nikolas are going to stay put for a while."

"Oh, so do I!" Alex murmured fervently. "Did you get my postcards?"

"Uh-huh. You liked Melbourne the best?"

"Mmmm. I think part of it was that we were there for nearly eight weeks. At least I had time to unpack! And I like doing master classes."

Alex stretched and lifted her heavy hair off the back of her neck. "Is it really a quarter to twelve?"

"Uh-huh. What time did you two get in?"

"It must have been after five. Pieter had invited a number of friends in for a late supper after the concert." Alex frowned and leaned back against the pillows. Her father had been in a strange mood last night. He was always volatile, but last night his spirits seemed to drop to new lows one minute and then soar to even greater heights of euphoria the next. She had been worried about him and had urged him to leave a number of times—which he definitely had not appreciated. Only after Pieter himself had insisted did he relent.

"Ruthy, would you go check and see if Nikolas is up yet? I've never known him to oversleep like this."

"All right, Alex, but I'm just going to take a peek. If he's not awake, I'm not going to disturb him. He's not getting any younger, you know, and he probably needs the rest after all the traipsing around you two have been doing."

After Ruthy had gone, treading out of the room with her firm, purposeful strides, Alex pushed aside the covers and crossed to the window to pull the drapes. It was a lovely April day, and looking down on Boston Common, Alex could see that the willows were already a bright green and the forsythia bushes were in full bloom. Here it was spring, she mused, and she hadn't had a winter this year! Their tour had taken them primarily into the Southern Hemisphere. Christmas had been spent in Sydney during the height of a summer heat wave.

For a moment she watched the boys playing baseball in the distance. It would be nice to have a few spare minutes just to walk around the Common, but it looked as though the day were pretty much scheduled for them if they were to see Pieter at three. What plans had he made for them next? Futilely Alex hoped that there would be at least a month of rest, but then, Nikolas never rested, not even when they were in residence in Boston. He always managed to find classes to teach, lectures to deliver, parties to attend, not to mention the endless hours of practice and rehearsal. And Pieter had mentioned something last night about a concert with the symphony and a new record contract. Once she wondered how Nikolas endured the pace. But *endured* was not the right word. He positively thrived on it, constantly driven with that restless energy.

"He's still sleeping sound as a baby, Alex," Ruthy said behind her. "But you come along and have something to eat before it's ruined."

It wasn't until an hour later that Alex began to be worried. Never had she known her father to sleep past noon, and now it was after one. He'd had quite a bit to drink the night before, but surely not enough to have this effect on him.

Nervously she bit her lip, not quite sure what to do. She didn't relish the thought of waking him if he indeed had intended to sleep on, but neither did she want to bear the brunt of his ill temper if he missed the meeting with Pieter. She would wait until two, she decided, and then if he still wasn't up, she'd have to wake him.

A half hour later she tiptoed to the door of his room and knocked lightly. Nothing. Carefully she opened the door a crack. In the dim light she could see him stretched out under the covers. He must have been exhausted. Alex very nearly closed the door again, deciding to call Pieter and postpone the meeting, and then something in the tenor of the room's quiet caught her attention. It was too quiet, too still. Her concern hardened into a cold fear as she walked silently and reluctantly to the side of the bed. Even before she touched him, she knew.

Nikolas Stephanos was dead.

In the nightmarish days that followed, Alex didn't know what she would have done without Pieter. He was the first person she called, and from then on she was able to leave everything in his capable hands. Pieter arrived with the doctor, and then events followed one after the other, almost too quickly for Alex's numb mind to comprehend. Funeral arrangements were made, friends contacted, the concerts canceled. Calls poured in by the hundreds, and Pieter supplied a secretary to cope with the voluminous mail, flowers, expressions of sympathy, the press.

Three days later, it was all over. Nikolas Stephanos was laid to rest in a quiet grave beside his parents, wife, and only sister. Tears ran unchecked down Alex's face as she stood beside the open grave. He was gone. The brilliant, tempermental musical genius Nikolas Stephanos was gone. And more, much more, than that, her father—the man who for over twenty-four years had given her life meaning and direction—was gone. The bottom had dropped out of Alex's world.

"We must talk, Alexandra."

Alex turned away from the window to where Pieter sat on the black velvet sofa in the living room.

"I still can't believe it, Pieter. Any moment I expect to hear him calling from the study. It—it all happened so fast! He was in his prime!"

"The doctor said he must have been living on reserves for a long time now. He burnt himself out. But at least you have the satisfaction of knowing that he did not suffer. The doctor believes that the heart attack came in his sleep. And he died at home, after a night of unequaled triumph. No musician could ask for more."

"Pieter, he—he kissed my hand that last

night. Do you—do you think he knew? Do you think he had been ill before and never told me?"

"It could be, child. It would not have been his way to have stopped, to have given up his music—not even if it meant his death."

"Do you know, Pieter, that last night was the first time in my life I felt that perhaps Nikolas cared about me—as anything but a musician, I mean."

"He loved you, my dear, in his own way," Pieter said quietly. "Perhaps that love was not the same kind as you and I might give another person—I do not believe he was capable of that—but he loved you. When your mother died, I saw all need and desire for human entanglements go from him. Music became his love, his life. Fortunately, you fit into that life because you, too, had a great potential which he could recognize, appreciate, develop. Many was the time he told me how proud he was of you."

"Do—do you mean that, Pieter?" Alex's mouth quivered, and she bit her bottom lip to stop its trembling.

"Have you ever known me to be anything but honest with you, child?"

Mutely Alex shook her head, too moved to speak.

"But now," Pieter continued briskly, clearing the lump from his throat, "we must talk about you, about your plans for the future."

Alex sighed and took a place beside him on

the couch. "What am I going to do? Am I going to tour on my own?"

"Isn't that the question I should be asking you?" the impresario murmured as he lifted a coffee cup to his lips.

"Hmmm?" she asked vaguely.

"Never mind. Tell me, Alexandra, do you ask me about your future as your manager or as your friend?"

She shrugged, not really understanding the question, and turned her head against the cushion of the couch to study his face. "As both, I guess. Is one different from the other?"

"Poor little Alexandra! That you should have to ask! Your music lessons, your career, all the people you have known and worked with professionally—these have been the sum total of your life, have they not? Do you know, old fool that I am, it was not until Nikolas died that I gave any thought to your having a life apart from the concert stage. But now I ask you, Alexandra. What do *you* wish to do with your life?"

Her soft brown eyes mirrored her bewilderment, and she found his question disturbing. "I—I've never thought about it. Music has been my life, as you said. From the time I was old enough to sit on the piano stool, I've known the shape my destiny would take."

"Your destiny, or your father's ambitions for you, my dear? But are those ambitions *your* ambitions? Now, if you had your choice, what would you do?"

Alex moved restlessly on the couch and nervously played with the button on her black silk suit. "I—I don't know if I can answer that."

"Come, come, child!" he persisted impatiently. "Have you never daydreamed? Have you never envisioned another way of life? Have you never thought of marriage, a home, children?"

A wry smile broke over Alex's face and she laughed weakly. "Oh, Pieter! When have I ever been allowed the indulgence of fruitless dreams?"

"Ah, Alex, Alex!" Pieter sighed sadly, shaking his mane of white hair. "Nikolas and I, both of us, we have done you a great disservice, have we not? We robbed you of your childhood, your growing-up years, and now you tell me we have even robbed you of your dreams!"

"Nonsense!" Alex laughed. "You make it sound as though my father kept me chained to the piano! Never, not even as a child, did he have to force me to practice. The music I made was all I ever needed to make me happy."

"Perhaps one does not miss what one has never had," Pieter murmured cryptically.

"Music is my life! It has always been!"

"But not in the same way that it consumed your father, I think," he observed shrewdly. "And that is what we must discuss."

What Alex read in his face made her suddenly uneasy. She had the oddest sensation that she was being cut adrift from the mooring that had anchored her all her young life. "You are trying to tell me something, Pieter," she said soberly. "What is it?"

He didn't answer for a moment, and when he finally spoke, his voice was thoughtful. "You are what now? Twenty-four? Twenty-five?"

"Twenty-five in August, as you well know."

"And no one can doubt your skill as a pianist. You play with technical mastery. Yes, and at times with great passion but—"

"But what?" Alex was shaken. Never had Pieter expressed any reservations or doubts about her work.

"But I am not sure you have what it takes to be a success as a solo performer on the concert circuit," he said ruthlessly.

"You—you think I'm not good enough?" she asked humbly, never doubting his right to make such a judgment. Tightly she clasped her hands in her lap to stop their trembling.

"Child, child! I did not say that! I said that you did not have what it takes to tour! I did not say that you did not have the talent."

"I—I don't think I understand, Pieter."

Her velvet brown eyes met his watery blue ones, and he saw the hurt and puzzlement there and laid his hand over hers.

"You and Nikolas toured together for what? Over four years? Yes? Tell me, Alexandra, in all truth. If it had not been for your father,

24

would you have willingly lived at such a pace? Would you have gone on month after month, from city to city, living out of a suitcase, with no real home, no real friends? Would you have done all that if it hadn't been for Nikolas's drive and his ambitions for you?"

Alex needed no time to consider her answer. She was so tired, so tired, just as he had known. "No," she said quietly. "No, I would not have lived like that—at least not all the time."

"What you lack, child, is not talent. Given more time and experience, you have the ability—genius, if you will—to rank with the greatest. What you lack is the need within you that drives a performer onward, seeking new audiences, new heights of acclaim. The great performers—I did not say artists—have the obsession to share their art with others, to feel the need in the audience that must be satisfied. They take the spark of expectation from the public and turn it into a fire. For them, the music must be a shared experience between audience and artist."

"And—and you don't think I have that need?" She knew that the description fit her father perfectly, but did it fit her? She didn't know.

"Many is the time I have watched you play, Alexandra. I can tell that you love the music to the depths of your soul, but for you the playing is a personal ritual, a desire to satisfy the longings inside yourself alone. You become so absorbed in the music that you are almost resentful at the end, when the applause draws you out of your mood. Your music *itself* is sufficient for you. The playing alone fulfills you—not the pleasure that you are capable of giving to others, the praise, the adulation. To meet the arduous demands of touring, you have to enjoy that life, or at the very least get personal satisfaction from it. And for you, too, the money to be made is immaterial. Nikolas has left you enough to live on for the rest of your life. He loved the touring, and while you played with him his ambitions and needs were enough to carry you along."

Alex could not deny the truth of what he said. Her pale face looked bewildered and faintly haunted, and when she spoke it was almost to herself. "But what will I do?"

"Despite these limitations, you are still a fine artist, and, as your manager, I would say that now is the right time to strike out on your own as a performer. Your name is well known and respected. I would have no trouble at all getting you bookings, record contracts, and keeping you in the public eye."

"But you just said—"

"Hear me out, Alexandra. I said, as your manager, that is what I would advise. But now I speak as I would to the daughter I never had. You are not happy, child. The last tour was very hard on you. You are much too thin, and you are living on your nerves." Tenderly he squeezed her tightly clasped hands and continued gently. "Take some time away. Find a way to live at a slower pace for a while. Allow yourself time to think, to dream if you will, to decide for yourself what will make you happy."

"But, Pieter," she interrupted desperately, "I don't know what I would do with myself! I'm not sure I would know how to live any other way, at least for long."

"No, you have never learned how to relax and have fun, have you, child?" Pieter said sadly. "To shop or go to the hairdresser's or a movie. You have never had a young man or done a thousand and one other things that are normal to a woman of your age. But you must learn, Alexandra. I would not see your talent wasted, but neither would I see you sacrifice your life to that talent."

"Like Nikolas?" she asked sadly.

"Yes, like Nikolas."

"Then what will I do?" She was both frightened and excited at the thought of such freedom.

Pieter paused for a moment, his keen eyes assessing her thoughtfully. "I have a suggestion. You may not like it, but I think it would be a perfect solution for you until you decide."

Alex laughed nervously. "I have the feeling you are about to suggest something terrible. You're much too cautious in your approach!"

"Not so terrible, and really you would be

doing me a favor." He paused again, and a mischievous smile broke over his face. "How would you like to go to Mexico?"

"Mexico? But why?"

"You have heard about Marcos Rivera? You know he had . . . an accident?"

"I didn't know until the other day that something was wrong. I saw an article in the paper saying he had had an operation. What happened?"

"Six months ago the fingers on his left hand were crushed," van Loos said bluntly. "The doctors now give him no hope that he will ever regain their full use. He will never play— at least as he did—again."

"But that's terrible!" Alex gasped, stunned by the news.

Pieter's voice was filled with anger as he replied harshly. "It *is* terrible! For anyone to lose the use of his hand is a tragedy, but for Marcos it is a catastrophe!"

"What—what has this to do with me?" she prompted as Pieter fell into a thoughtful silence.

"You, Alexandra, could help him, if you would."

"I? How?"

"For the past two years Marcos has been composing. At the time of the accident he was working on a major piece—a suite for piano. I saw him last week. I was with him when he left the hospital. He is a strong man, and he's bitter but not defeated. He wants to go back to his composing, and I am trying to convince him that what he needs is a pianist, someone who can play the music as he writes it." He paused and looked into her startled face. "Would you be willing to be that person?"

"You want *me* to work with Marcos Rivera?"

"Why not you? You have met him, have you not?"

"You should remember, Pieter. You introduced me to him in London when I was sixteen."

"And you were so tongue-tied that you could not even speak." He laughed. "You looked at him as if he were a god who deigned to smile on a lowly mortal!"

"He was!"

"Not a god, child. Just a man, and the gods have played a cruel trick on him. He is wounded and in pain. Not a pain of the physical body—that is healing. It is a pain of the soul. And you could help him, I know."

Alex sat in thoughtful silence. The whole suggestion seemed incredible. That Marcos Rivera, the genius whom—yes, she admitted it to herself—whom she had hero-worshiped, whose career she had followed so religiously for eight years, should have need of her talents! The whole notion seemed absurd!

"Are you sure he would want me?" she asked meekly.

"No, I am not sure at all." Pieter chuckled. "He has the devil's own temper, and when I left him he was still cursing . . . well, never mind! No, he may not *want* you, but he *needs* you."

"You certainly paint an attractive picture!" Alex gasped.

"You will soon win him over," Pieter said blithely. "You are used to working with a difficult man. Marcos can be no worse than Nikolas ever was. And your experience has taught you tact and an understanding of the problems of genius. Your personal qualifications are even greater than your professional."

Alex shuddered at the description Pieter offered. When he had first suggested she make a change in her life, she had not envisioned exchanging one tyrant for another!

Pieter's face softened as he accurately read her chagrin. "I am very fond of Marcos," he said gently. "I have known and worked with him for many years. He is still a young man, only thirty-five. It is too young to have his brilliant career snatched from him. He needs to channel his energies into his composing— and I can assure you that he is good! He must be made to see that his life still has purpose and meaning. Won't you help him?"

"Will you give me a little time to think it over? I still can't believe it!"

He patted her hand and pushed himself to his feet. "Of course. Take a day or two to consider. But I think a few months in Mexico would do you the world of good, also."

Mexico! She knew it was Marcos Rivera's native country, though his mother had been American.

"The work would not be strenuous," Pieter added coaxingly, "and the house is very secluded, on a remote part of the west coast. You would find plenty of time to get the rest you need."

"May I call you tomorrow?"

"Of course."

Long after Pieter had gone, Alex sat on the couch, lost in thought. The apartment seemed so quiet, even with the faint sounds of Ruthy puttering around in the kitchen. Never had she felt so all alone. Nikolas had never been a companion in the accepted sense of the word, but he had been a presence, and his personality had filled the rooms of the apartment with a tangible energy. In all the years they had traveled together, played together, there had been no easy rapport, no exchange of thoughts and feelings, but still she missed him dreadfully even though he had died almost a stranger to her—remote and impersonal.

On an impulse Alex threw a jacket around her shoulders and slipped out of the old brownstone house to the Common across the street. The afternoon was mild. Mothers were out with their children, old men sat idle on the benches, and a group had gathered around a young man strumming a banjo.

Alex went unnoticed in the crowd of people, and she liked the feeling of anonymity in the public park. Here, she thought with a smile, she was just Alex Stephens, out-of-work musician. No rehearsals awaiting her, no plane to catch, no concert to perform. The freedom was intoxicating! But she was also wise enough to know that it would soon pass.

She began to give serious consideration to what Pieter's suggestion would mean. Mexico! Marcos Rivera!

If ever she had had any adolescent dreams, they had all woven themselves around this man, but that had been years before. Now, to have the chance to see him again, to work with him! The thought was staggering. She had the strange feeling that she was on the verge of a new life, that here was the opportunity to make a new beginning.

For the first time in three days, the numbness that had gripped her faded and her depression lifted. Marcos Rivera! If she could help him, put her talents at his disposal, it would give her own life new purpose.

Yes! She would do it! But not as Alexandra Stephanos. That was the past, at least for a while. She would call Pieter tomorrow and tell him she would go, but only as Alex Stephens. Alexandra Stephanos had her life clearly charted for her. To Alex Stephens— anything could happen!

Chapter Two

$\mathcal{O}$ n a warm, humid day in late April, Alex landed in Mexico. From Guadalajara she took a small charter plane to Tepic, the nearest city of any size to San Blas—the coastal village where Marcos Rivera now made his home. Pieter had made all the arrangements for her trip, even to hiring a car and driver to meet her at the airport in Tepic for the final leg of her long journey.

"*Buenos días, señorita!* I am Juan!" the driver introduced himself cheerfully as he helped her into the back of his ancient, ramshackle Chevrolet. "This car go like a bomb," he called as he dumped her luggage in the trunk. "I get you to San Blas real quick!"

"Not too quick, I hope," Alex muttered as she sank back into the seat. Her hope was not to be realized, as a few moments later Juan raced the engine, honked his way into traffic, and tore off down the road at a pace that kept Alex clutching the edge of her seat.

"It is a beautiful day," he offered, grinning,

as he bowled along the Mazatlán, highway. As they traveled he kept up a running commentary, half in English, half in Spanish, on the landscape, the people, and any other topic that caught his roving interest. Once Alex saw that little response was necessary from her to keep him going, she followed him with only half an ear as her thoughts drifted on to the meeting ahead with Marcos Rivera.

She was looking forward to seeing him again, though she imagined there would be some tension at first. Pieter had contacted him, explaining that he had found a pianist ideal for Marcos's work. A week had gone by before Pieter had informed her that Rivera had confirmed the arrangements. Alex shrewdly suspected that the pianist's acquiescence in the matter had involved a certain amount of coercion on Pieter's part, but she frankly preferred not to know the details.

The week before her departure she had spent in the unaccustomed pleasure of shopping for new clothes. Her previous wardrobe had consisted of very expensive, beautifully tailored clothes—all of her father's choosing—in styles and colors more suited to a middle-aged matron than a modern young woman. Left to her own devices, she chose bright prints and vivid colors that complemented her rich chestnut hair and creamy complexion and suited her own burgeoning taste. The results of her splurge were clothes such as she had never worn before—shorts and brief tops, slacks and cool, dainty blouses, sundresses that left her arms and shoulders exposed, several swimsuits much more revealing than any she had ever owned, and shimmering, floating evening dresses (though she really had no reason to suppose she would need them) in colorful silks and chiffons. She never wanted to have to dress in tailored suits and black crêpe gowns again!

The day before she was due to leave Boston, she had screwed up her courage and put herself in the hands of an expert hairdresser. Gone now was the prim, sedate chignon she had worn since she was a teenager. The man had left her hair long in back, merely trimming and shaping it, but the front he had cut so it curled and feathered away from her face, giving her prominent cheekbones, gaunt cheeks, and full, generous mouth a lovely, soft vulnerability that made her feel intensely feminine—and she enjoyed the feeling. She took great satisfaction from the fact that when she had gone to see Pieter to say good-bye, the metamorphosis was so complete he hadn't recognized her. Yes, Alex Stephens was alive and well and on her way to Mexico!

After a half hour, Juan turned off the smooth highway onto a twisting, narrow road that led through the thick jungle terrain. The countryside was wild and sparsely settled. Here and there banana groves and farmland had been carved out of the lush undergrowth. The farmers' houses were little more than thatch-roofed shacks thrown together on the edge of the trees. It was a beautiful, primitive area very unlike the desert of the north part of the country or the sprawling cities that Alex had visited before.

Twenty miles later they emerged from the trees on the brow of a hill, and below them lay the village of San Blas nestled along the sandy coast of the azure Pacific. Juan stopped at the village *zocolo* to ask questions, and Alex peered with interest at the quaint market square. At one end stood a neat white stucco church. At the other end were the stalls and tents erected to display the local wares—fruits, vegetables, woven baskets of unbelievable variety, brightly colored blankets and clothing.

"A little farther on," Juan indicated as he climbed back into the driver's seat.

Just past the last of the houses, he slowed and crept alongside a high stone wall covered with vines and blooming wisteria. Even searching carefully he nearly missed the driveway leading up to *Casa de Rivera*. The gate was open but the entrance was almost obscured by bushes and hanging vines. The narrow lane, scarcely more than a rutted dirt road, wound through the dense undergrowth and had obviously seen little traffic recently. Bushes scraped the sides of the large American car, and Juan had to slow to a crawl to cope with the deep holes in the road.

"Juan, are you sure this is the right place?"

Alex asked nervously as the front tire hit a particularly deep hole.

"Sí! Right place." Juan beamed cheerfully. "Look. Up ahead. The trees clear."

He was right. Not too much farther on, the lush foliage gave way to what must have once been lawn but now looked more like a hayfield. High, swaying palms lined both sides of a long, circular drive that curved in front of a large stucco structure, covered with climbing and flowering vines. Railed balconies faced out from the upper story, and the red-tiled roof peeped through the trees.

Juan increased his speed now that the end was in sight and bumped and jolted his way along the remaining distance until he screeched to a halt at the broad, shallow steps that led to a pillared archway in the center of the house.

Slowly Alex climbed, bruised and shaken, out of the back seat and stared incredulously at the sight. Her first vague suspicions now hardened into certainty. The place was a ruin! The entire north wing of the house, roofless and windowless, was quickly being reclaimed by the encroaching jungle. Small animals scurried into hiding as she approached the steps. Not a soul was in sight. Surely this couldn't be the place!

"I find someone to help with the luggage. Be back in a jiffy!" Juan called and disappeared into the shrubs at the south end of the house. Gingerly Alex walked up the wide front steps, trying to avoid the loose and broken tiles. The entrance to the building was through the archway and across a large interior courtyard. In the center of the open space was a beautifully tiled fountain, from the looks of it long defunct. The bronze statue in the middle was blue and green from moss and corrosion, and the water in the pool was stagnant and filled with slime, decaying vegetation, and dead insects.

Alex shuddered delicately and looked around, unsure what to do next, wishing that Juan hadn't gone off and left her. Should she call out or knock? Ahead of her in the central portion of the house were large studded oak doors, but the bar across them was certainly not welcoming. There were two other entrances to the courtyard—doorless arches set into the side wings that led to covered passage ways and smaller courtyards—but Alex had no inclination to explore these. Obviously, Juan had made a mistake. The house was derelict, and the sooner they could get back into town and make further inquiries, the better. It was getting late, and already the sun was beginning to edge toward the horizon, throwing most of the courtyard into shadow. The second-story balcony that ran along three sides even now looked dark and ominous. Perspiration trickled down the back of her neck, and she smoothed a stray wisp of hair back away from her face.

Where on earth had Juan disappeared to?

She was about to return to the car and wait when she heard footsteps coming along one of the interior passages. Before she could tell from which direction the sound came, the footsteps stopped and a voice cracked through the incessant hum of insects and the cry of the birds.

"Who the devil are you!"

Alex swung around and narrowed her eyes in the direction of the voice. She could just make out the tall, broad figure of a man standing in the shadow of one of the arches. Her first impulse was to turn and run, but common sense told her that the man must be Marcos Rivera. His face was in shadow, but when he moved a step closer and stood legs astride, hands on his hips, a heavily bandaged left hand confirmed his identity.

His sudden appearance, coupled with his unfriendly reception, kept her silent as his eyes narrowed and slowly examined her taut figure with more annoyance than pleasure. He had addressed her first in Spanish, but now he switched to faultless English.

"I said, who are you? Is that your car?"

His voice was harsh and abrupt, clearly showing his irritation. He took another step forward into the light, and Alex had her second shock. This was definitely Marcos Rivera, but where was the charming, cultured man she remembered? This formidable stranger, dressed in full-sleeved muslin peasant shirt and white pants stuffed negligently into black riding boots, looked for all the world like a throwback to some bygone age. Beyond a superficial similarity, she was hard put to recognize the man she had met so long ago.

His black hair was ruffled, falling carelessly across his forehead. His chiseled bronze face was much thinner, and now there was no smile to soften the hard line of his jaw or give warmth to the cold jade green of his eyes—the only sign of his mixed parentage. No longer the international cosmopolitan, he appeared untamed and slightly dangerous. In spite of the heat of the day, Alex shivered.

"Señor Rivera?" Alex asked hesitantly.

"Well, well! The lady has a tongue in her head, after all!" he drawled nastily. "What are you? A reporter? Well, you've wasted your time! You can climb into that pile of junk at the front and get out the same way you came in! I don't know how you found this place anyway," he muttered as he turned back toward the arched doorway. He was going to leave!

"No, wait!" she called, hurrying after him. "You don't understand!"

"My good woman, it is you who do not understand. I do not receive visitors. Now leave!"

He had paused momentarily in his retreat, and Alex would have reached him if her toe hadn't caught on a broken tile.

"Ohhh!" With a cry she was down.

She heard him curse quietly but very effectively before he swung around to haul her roughly up by one arm and stand her on her feet. Her hand was scraped and blood was trickling down from a cut on her knee. Her pale blue dress was torn at the waist and covered with dirt where she had fallen on the filthy tiles. But Marcos Rivera seemed neither to notice nor to care.

"Now get out before something worse happens to you!" he spat through clenched teeth. "I did not invite you here! You are trespassing!"

"Oh, but you did! Invite me here, that is." She laughed shakily, trying to regain her composure.

"What are you talking about?" Alex had taken hold of his arm to steady herself, and through the thin fabric of his shirt she could feel his muscles tense. He was like a large, lithe jungle cat, poised to spring. "What did you mean by that?" he repeated, shaking her slightly, and his hold tightened on her wrist until she thought he would snap it in two.

Standing so close to him, Alex had to look a long way up into his stern face as she gasped and stuttered, "P-Pieter van Loos told you I was coming."

"Pieter!" His face went pale under his tan. "Who are you?"

"I—I am Alex Stephens."

"Impossible!"

He pulled away from her as though her touch revolted him. Quickly she backed away until the edge of the fountain halted her retreat. Had his accident unsettled his mental balance? Slowly he advanced on her, his eyes blazing like green jewels.

"Now tell me who you are and why you are here!" His tone was cold and menacing.

"I told you!" Alex cried. "I'm Alex Stephens. Mr. van Loos sent me." Reaching into her handbag, she pulled out an envelope and handed it to him. "Here is a letter of introduction, if you don't believe me."

"Impossible," he murmured again, scanning the contents of Pieter's letter. "Pieter would not do this to me!"

"What's wrong? Why—why don't you believe me?" Alex stammered.

"Because Alex Stephens is a man!" Rivera stated baldly. "Pieter knows I would never allow a woman to come here!"

"Ohhh, I see!" Alex exclaimed on a long, released breath. For the first time since his sudden appearance she relaxed. He had expected a man, and for someone who was trying to protect his privacy, her appearance must have come as a shock—not that that entirely excused his rudeness to her.

"I don't particularly care what you see or don't see," he was continuing. "I won't have you here! Now get out!"

At first Alex had been amused by the mistake, but twelve hours of travel had dulled her sense of humor. If there was a mix-up—and she didn't doubt there was—she knew exactly where to place the blame. Pieter had for some reason of his own deliberately led Marcos Rivera to believe that Alex Stephens was male. She was certainly competent to do the job, and no high-handed male chauvinist was going to tell her differently! Did he believe that women were useful for only one purpose?

She had read enough in the papers about his personal life to know he was no woman-hater. The women who had been seen in his company over the years were legion. Yet there was no mistaking the darkly hostile gleam in his eye as he tapped his foot impatiently, waiting for her to leave.

What to do? She certainly had no intention of getting back into that car with the lead-footed Juan, no matter what! And besides, she had promised Pieter that she would make every effort to overlook what he had called Marcos's idiosyncrasies—a misnomer if there ever was one! Violent dislike would have been a better term!

"Señor Rivera," she said into the silence, "I was hired in your behalf by Mr. van Loos, with your full knowledge and approval. I have traveled nearly four thousand miles to get here. Can you give me one good reason why I should leave now?"

From the look on his face he could undoubtedly have given her a dozen personal reasons, but he chose the most apparent. "Look around you, Miss Stephens! I would say that what you see should be reason enough!"

"I hardly think you work among the wreckage. Surely there must be some part of this—this ruin that's habitable!"

"A very small part," he snapped. "And I don't intend to have a woman underfoot day and night!"

"Underfoot! I came here to work, not to run around like a—a house pet!"

His gritted teeth indicated he was keeping a rein on his uncertain temper only with the greatest difficulty. "I live here alone with only a manservant."

"Then perhaps you would be kind enough to instruct him to show me to a room. You knew someone was coming, so something must have been prepared," she retorted dryly.

Still he did not move, but she could see indecision in his eyes now. Suddenly her shoulders slumped. She was so tired, and the past few minutes of tension had not helped. "Please, señor," she said more quietly, and in spite of herself her voice quavered a little. "I'm hot and I'm tired and I'm dirty." She glanced down at her injured knee. "And I'm bleeding!"

His muttered oath was more distinct this time, but she didn't know whether he cursed her, himself, or Pieter.

"All right!" he snapped at last. "Come with me and I'll get you bandaged up. We'll sort this out inside."

He turned on his heel, not waiting to see if she followed, and Alex limped quickly after him. Once through the archway, he suddenly stopped so abruptly that she nearly knocked into him. "Wait here," he ordered. "I'll go through the house and unlock this door so you don't have to walk around."

He strode off without a backward glance, and Alex leaned weakly against the doorframe, wondering vaguely if he would even bother to come back. It was almost dark now, but the air was still very warm and heavy with the fragrance of the flowers that climbed the walls of the small courtyard where she waited. What an unfortunate beginning!

"Señorita Stephens!"

From a covered passageway the burly form of her driver emerged. "Over here, Juan."

"I just see the señor. He say I'm to wait and take you back with me tonight."

"That won't be necessary, Juan," she said with more assurance than she was feeling. "I'm staying, so you can go on." As she opened her purse to pull out a bill, she had the odd sensation of burning her boats behind her. "This is for you. Thank you very much."

"*Muchas gracias!*" His hand closed eagerly over the money. "I have your luggage inside."

He had just disappeared into the adjoining courtyard when the door beside her creaked. The hinges were obviously rusty, and Marcos Rivera had to put his shoulder to it to push it wide enough for her to enter.

"Well, come in, come in!" he said crossly.

Silently Alex eased through the narrow

opening and followed him across a broad, dark hallway to the room beyond. A kerosene lantern stood on a table, throwing a circle of light around a small area. The rest of the huge room was in darkness.

"Sit down!" he ordered, indicating a rotting velvet sofa. "Tomás will be here in a minute with something to fix your leg and a drink."

At first Alex perched gingerly on the edge of the dusty cushion, then she relaxed back. Her dress could hardly get in worse condition than it was already, she thought dryly. Rivera made no effort to initiate a conversation but sat opposite her on a high-backed wooden chair, studying her in speculative silence. The sofa was built on massive lines and made Alex's slight frame appear even more fragile. The lantern brought out the copper highlights in her dark hair but made dark pools of her eyes and hollows in her cheeks. Just for a moment she closed her eyes and missed the flicker of compunction that softened his hard gaze before his lips tightened.

"Pieter must have been mad to send a child on this wild escapade!" he suddenly exploded. "Has he become senile?"

A smile played around the corners of Alex's soft mouth. "He wouldn't thank you for that. Nor do I. I'm no child. I'm twenty-four."

Whatever comment he would have made was silenced by the arrival of his manservant. Tomás was full-blooded Indian, thin and wrinkled with age. After one swift look at Alex, he addressed the younger man in a rapid Spanish, too quick for Alex's tired brain to follow. Rivera muttered something sharply in return, and the servant shrugged, set the tray he carried on the table, and left. Once he was gone, Rivera handed Alex a tall, cool glass of fruit punch.

"Here. Drink this, and I'll attend to your knee."

Impatiently he tore away the tattered remains of her nylons and exposed the wound. One-handed, he wrung out a clean towel in the basin of water and began cleaning away the dirt.

With his attention directed to her injured leg, Alex had a chance to study him at leisure. Looking down on his bent head, she saw the first smatterings of silver running through the dark hair. The lines in his forehead and around his eyes were very faint, though deep grooves were cut along his straight nose and around the firm, taut lips. The charm he had once possessed was gone, but he was still the most devastatingly attractive man she had ever met. She shrugged away the thought and concentrated her gaze on his hand. His fingers were just as she imagined—long, supple, and strong. He must have a reach of an octave and three, at least, she mused idly.

At that moment he brought up his injured hand to hold the gauze in place as he applied the tape with the other, and Alex's soft heart was wrung at the sight of that immobilized hand. It was such a crime! Such a waste of musical genius! For the first time since her arrival she really considered her mission here, and she felt a renewed sense of purpose. She would stay, and she would help him— whether at this moment he wanted her or not!

"There!" he said, straightening in his chair and reaching for his own glass. "Now we can talk."

"You've recovered from the shock of finding that I am a woman?" she asked lightly, her emotions still stirred by his injured hand.

"I didn't mean to be . . . offensive," he answered coolly, "but you must see that this is no place for a woman. I run a bachelor establishment of the most primitive kind." He smiled an unpleasant, cynical smile. "For the time being, this rotting ruin suits my mood, but I could not ask any woman to live like this."

"So you mean to send me away," she murmured, watching him carefully.

"I can't!" he said harshly. "That is the point."

"What do you mean you can't?" Alex asked, startled.

"I mean that when I talked with Pieter, I gave him my solemn promise that I would keep Alex Stephens here, no matter what, for at least a month's trial. I see now," he said dryly, "why Pieter was so insistent on extracting the promise from me."

"And do you intend to keep your word?" she asked curiously.

"Are you questioning my honor?" he snapped. "I have no choice!" He paused and sent her a calculating look. "But you do! Who could blame you—certainly not van Loos—if you found the conditions here unendurable? You have only to tell him the manner in which I live, and he can find someone . . . well, more suitable."

"Which euphemism translates to someone male," she said dryly.

His voice suddenly became more gentle and persuasive. "Look at you. You are five foot four of nothing but skin and bones. Life here is hard. The climate is hot and humid. There are no other women in the house. The nearest town of any size is nearly two hours' drive away. There are no shops, no movies, no television. You would die of boredom."

"We would have the work." Alex's reply was deceptively mild, but her chin was raised and a look came into her eye that Pieter would have recognized as being very much like her father's flinty determination.

"Well, I do not intend to begin working with a woman who will not be able to last out the week!"

"Oh, I'll last much longer than that, I assure you!"

"And you couldn't possibly have the necessary musical experience," he was stung into replying.

Alex had taken philosophically the aspersions on her appearance, her character, her stamina, but she would not allow aspersions on her ability as a musician. "Do you always base judgments on such slight evidence?" she asked coldly. "Do you really believe that P—Mr. van Loos would have sent you an incompetent?"

"I think he might have been persuaded by a pair of big brown eyes," he drawled. "I don't need someone who can just play the notes. I need someone who can *feel* my music, understand the demands of a concert work. Where have you played? Recitals at some conservatory?"

A temper Alex didn't even know she possessed brought the blood to her face, and for a moment she was tempted to tell this arrogant man who she really was. Recitals indeed! Then reason took over. She didn't want to trade on her name. She wanted the satisfaction of proving herself on her own merits and would derive a great deal of satisfaction from making him eat those words.

"Oh, I play professionally. I've even managed to make a living at it," she said sweetly.

"Doing what? Playing in church?" he sneered.

A hint of mischief gleamed in her eyes. Insufferable man! Here went Pieter's confidence in her tact. She would really give him something to chew over. "Yes, church certainly. And I play at weddings and funerals. That's on the side, of course. I've been earning my living playing in a night club in Boston." Choke over that one, Señor Rivera!

And he did. "A nightclub!" he sputtered.

"Oh, very high class." she said airily, embroidering on her theme. "Only the very best people. Of course, it is rather annoying when people try to talk over the music." She shrugged artistically. "That's why I found Pieter's proposition that I come here so appealing. I wouldn't dream of missing this opportunity to work with a real musician."

She paused and waited for his anger to explode over her head, but he merely clenched his good fist and gritted his teeth.

"So, you have no intention of leaving!"

"Of course not," she said innocently, opening her eyes wide. "And don't worry about the accommodations. I find your house . . . er . . . rustic. And quite fascinating. Could I see my room now?"

For several moments he continued to glare at her, his mind in high gear, and then a sardonic smile twisted the corner on one lip. "If you insist. . . . Tomás!"

The man appeared so quickly that Alex knew he must have been hovering just down the hall.

"Señor?"

"Tomás," he said in English for her benefit,

"I am going to show Miss Stephens up to the gold room. You can bring her bags there. And dismiss her driver."

"He has already gone, señor. On señorita's orders."

Alex met Rivera's irate stare with a bland smile. He said something to his servant in a rapid, highly idiomatic Spanish that once again she couldn't follow, and the man shrugged, muttered under his breath, and disappeared into the gloom beyond the doorway.

"If you will follow me, Miss Stephens?" Rivera said with ironic politeness as he picked up the lantern and preceded her out the door.

They were soon in the entry hallway, a large round room rising two stories to a stained-glass dome in the ceiling that let in the last dying rays of the day. Their footsteps echoed on the tiles as they crossed to the staircase that encircled the room and disappeared out of sight on the upper level. The whole place smelled of mold and disuse, and not for the first time Alex wondered how a man who had appeared so fastidious could now endure living in such apparent squalor.

At the top of the stairs he turned into a long corridor that ran the length of the central part of the house.. They turned down another hallway, narrower than the first, that ran at right angles. Alex could now surmise that the house was shaped like a capital E and they were in the center wing. The threadbare car-

pet runner on the oak floor, the dust everywhere, the cobwebs that hung from the high
ceiling indicated that this floor was not used
now, and she could only assume that his own
rooms were on the floor below.

He led her to the far end of the hall before
opening one of the heavy oak doors. The room
they entered had indeed once been decorated
in gold, and the heavy velvet drapes hanging
at the long windows and surrounding the
ornate four-poster bed still showed streaks of
color in the yellow light of the lantern. But
Alex strongly suspected that in the cold light
of day they would appear mostly dirty gray.
What little furniture there was in the room
was under sheets that had turned yellow with
age. The dark wooden floor was carpetless
except for a few scattered throw rugs of inde-
terminate color. All in all, Alex concluded,
the room had the appeal of a mausoleum.

"We had prepared a room next to my own,"
Rivera offered by way of explanation, "but I
think this one will suit you better. Tomás will
make up the bed and clean while we eat."

It had better be a lengthy meal, Alex
thought dryly. It would take an army of servants working two days to put this room in
order. She doubted if it had been occupied
since the Mexican Revolution.

"There is a bathroom attached," he said,
indicating a door on the far side. "We've had a
lot of rain these past few weeks, so the taps
may work. If not, Tomás can bring you some

water up from the kitchen. We have a hand pump there."

A clatter in the hallway heralded Tomás's arrival with her luggage. From under his arm protruded two candelabra. Candles were sticking out of each of his pockets. He dumped the bags unceremoniously on the floor, whisked the covered sheet off a table in the middle of the room, and set up the candles.

"Tomás will try to hunt up another lantern, but these should do for tonight," her reluctant host said as he gave a final cursory glance around the room. "Shall we have dinner in an hour? If you can find your way back down to the hall, I'll meet you there."

"I bring up some towels with the rest of the cases," Tomás muttered. "Water, too."

"Thank you very much," Alex said sweetly, smiling at the two glowering men. "I'll see you in an hour, then."

Once they had gone, she took a branch of candles and held it high over her head to see the room better. It must have been quite lovely in its day. One entire wall was lined with built-in cupboards whose doors were ornate and beautifully carved. What furniture there was in the room—only a table and a few chairs—was old and scratched but serviceable. The bed dominated most of the room. It must have been six feet wide and eight feet, long.

Before she had a chance to explore any further, Tomás arrived with the rest of her luggage, towels, and a pitcher of water. Alex was on the verge of addressing him in her rusty but more than adequate Spanish when intuition made her change her mind.

"Thank you, Tomás. Where do I find you if I need anything else?"

"The bellrope work—sometimes. If I hear it, I will come. Señor, he say not to change for dinner unless you want to."

"Tell him thank you," she offered dryly, looking at her torn and dirty dress. "I won't be late. I'm starving!"

She was indeed very hungry. She had had lunch on the flight to Guadalajara and bought some fruit in Tepic, but that was long ago.

When Tomás had departed once again, she took the candles into the bathroom, and it was fortunate she was holding them tightly, for she nearly dropped them when she saw the scurry of insect life in the antiquated bathtub. Silverfish, cockroaches, and black beetles— some nearly two inches long—scampered and slithered toward the drain when the light hit them.

Her first impulse was to let out an outraged, bloodcurdling scream, but she squelched the very natural desire. In the first place, there was no one to hear her. In the second, if she did manage to make herself heard, she could imagine the cynical smirk she would receive from her host.

Gingerly she picked her way across the tiles to the sink, hoping that the bugs were limited to the bathtub and didn't have friends and relatives lurking all over the room. Experimentally she flushed the toilet and was relieved to see that it worked. But when she turned on the water tap in the sink, all she got was a thin, dark stream of brown, rusty water. So much for a good wash, she thought ruefully. Anyway, nothing could induce her to take a bath in that bathtub. Now or ever!

Retreating once more to the bedroom, she crossed to the windows and pulled back the heavy drapes. There she had her first pleasant surprise. She hadn't realized that the house was built right on the ocean, and her room was only about a hundred yards from the beach. The full-length windows opened onto a balcony, and; below, the moon glistened on the white sands that stretched for miles in either direction.

Later on, after dinner, she would blow out the candles so that they wouldn't attract any flying night life, open the windows, and listen to the sound of the water against the shore. The prospect excited her, and in spite of the tense time she had just had, the insects, and the grim thought of what other nasty surprises she was in for, she chuckled to herself.

It didn't take much imagination or shrewdness to figure out that Marcos Rivera was doing his best to get rid of her, and she suspected that this filthy, musty room was all a part of his plan to discourage her. But he had made a tactical error. Alex had lived most of her life in the impersonal sterility of dormitory rooms and hotel suites, and she was young and hearty enough to consider the *Casa de Rivera* an adventure. With some cleaning, airing, and insecticide this room would suit her just fine, and when she wanted to escape, the beach was only as far away as the back door.

But she would stay on guard. She had a definite suspicion that this was just the first of a series of ploys he would use to drive her away, but he had reckoned without the stubbornness she had inherited from her father.

Alex found her way down the stairs an hour later with no difficulty, for Tomás had lighted candles in wall sconces along the way. Her host was waiting for her in the hall as he had promised, pacing restlessly. Alex was glad that she had taken the time to change from her torn dress into something fresh, for despite his instructions to her, he himself had changed into black trousers and a silk shirt. His hair was now combed and he had shaved off the shadow of beard. Now he looked much more like the man she remembered, she thought, but took it back when he smiled. The derisive twist of his lips he turned on her held more than a bit of malice.

"Did you find everything in order?" he questioned innocently.

"Oh, yes!" Her voice betrayed nothing but

enthusiasm. "The view from my balcony is glorious! I can't wait to see it in the daytime."

That was obviously not the answer he expected, and Alex was delighted to see that she had managed to wipe that nasty smile from his face and bring a dark, glowering look to his eyes.

"Well, come on, then!" he snapped. "Tomás is serving dinner in the drawing room. The dining room isn't fit to live in."

A table had been opened near the window, and two places were already set. Tomás was still bringing in the wonderful-smelling food and setting it on a sideboard as they entered.

"Better eat before it gets any colder," the servant muttered, and Alex had the distinct impression that this wasn't the place where his master usually chose to eat. Did Rivera usually just have a tray in his workroom? she wondered.

He handed her a plate from the table and invited her to help herself, and something in his expression made her give a sharp look at the food. She could see nothing amiss. In fact, it looked quite wonderful. The entire meal was traditionally Mexican: enchiladas, nachos, chili relleno—much of the Mexican food she enjoyed most. Then she saw what was missing. Conspicuous by their absence were all the milder accoutrements to a meal— fruits, vegetables, salads, the bland refried beans. She knew from past experience that the food prepared for them was loaded with hot spices and the mouth-burning jalapeño peppers.

Her lips twitched in amusement. Not satisfied with making her lodging as uncomfortable as possible, Rivera was now going to try to either burn her out or starve her out, depending on the strength of her constitution. He couldn't know that over the course of her career she had spent several weeks at one time or another in Mexico and was well used to the food. In fact, traveling had, of necessity, given her an eclectic taste. Were she in fact the little-traveled city girl from Boston he thought her, she might have been daunted by the food.

"This smells marvelous," she offered brightly, helping herself to large quantities of the hot dishes. "I didn't realize how hungry I was." The only relief from the hot food was the platter of corn tortillas, and she took several.

"You like Mexican food?" he asked blandly as he heaped food on his own plate.

"I haven't had it before," she lied glibly. Why spoil his nasty little joke at the beginning? "But I'm sure I'll love it. It looks wonderful."

Alex saw his lips twitch before he controlled them, and she smiled innocently up at him as he seated her politely at the table. Once he joined her, Alex kept up a conversation of inconsequential chatter, nonchalantly clean ing her plate, careful to temper the hottest food with the bland tortillas. It gave her immense satisfaction to watch the puzzled frown gather in his eyes as amusement fled and his lips became set in a hard straight line. She nearly laughed aloud when Tomás returned and saw her empty plate. He met his master's eyes with a baffled stare and then shook his head in disbelief.

The wine served with dinner was excellent, but Alex put her hand over the glass when her host would have filled it a third time. She had a feeling she needed a clear head tonight if she was to deal with this difficult man. She would watch and listen carefully and see what information she could pick up about the man and his home.

Her opportunity came over coffee. Tomás had cleared away the dishes and left, only to return a few minutes later. "Señor," he said in Spanish, but this time slow enough for Alex to follow the conversation, "there is a call for you. Your aunt."

Rivera swore softly and then rose to his feet. "All right," he returned in his native language. "I'll take it in my study."

Oh, ho! Alex thought as he excused himself. So somewhere around was a telephone. Did that mean there were other modern conveniences lurking about? And compared to this dilapidated drawing room, *study* sounded like a nice, normal place. Also, she had seen no signs of a piano. There had to be a room where he worked. Maybe tomorrow she would find a way to explore the rest of the house, though she had a feeling that Tomás would be hard on her heels.

By the time Rivera returned, Alex was yawning. It had been a long, grueling day. He stood for a moment in the doorway looking in her direction, but Alex had the feeling he wasn't seeing her, and somehow she sensed that, for once, the ominous frown on his face was not aimed at her.

"I think I'll go to bed now, if you will excuse me," she said, rising to her feet. "What time do you want to start in the morning?"

"Hmmm?" he murmured vaguely, startled back to the present. "Oh, I thought I made it clear that we would not begin working until you made up your mind whether or not you wanted to stay," he stated coldly—and the frown was once more for her benefit.

"My mind is already made up, Señor Rivera. No, that's much too formal. Marcos!" she said sweetly. "It's you who have to become reconciled."

She ignored his expletive, but with her hand on the door she turned back again. "Then, until you give the word, my time is my own?"

"As long as you stay out of my way, I don't care what you do!" he snarled.

Give him a few days to get used to her, she thought optimistically, and then she would tackle him again. Patience had always been one of her virtues, after all.

Excusing herself politely, she made her way

back into the dimly lighted hall and up the stairs. What a perfect place for a horror film! she thought cheerfully as she passed a rusty suit of Spanish armor on the landing. All this house needed was a headless specter to float through the wall, and she looked hopefully at the cracked and peeling paint. Tomorrow she would explore some of the other rooms on her floor. Maybe she could find sliding panels and secret passageways. And when that got boring, she would swim and laze about on the beach.

The prospects for the coming days were so entrancing that she laughed happily to herself and took a skip down the hall, unsure whether it was the wine she had drunk or the heady sense of a newfound freedom that made her so lightheaded. Not even the dour, disapproving Marcos Rivera could dim this novel experience. She found him frightening and, yes, she admitted to herself, quite intimidating when he chose to turn his scathing tongue loose on her, but at the same time, after years of repression, this contest of wills, these verbal skirmishes, were tremendously exciting!

Pieter had been absolutely right about her coming to Mexico. This change was just what she needed to help assuage her grief and give her life a new perspective. For Alex, this was a voyage of discovery—mainly about herself. For one thing, she had never known before what a temper she had. And who would have dreamed that she would find so much enjoyment in foiling Marcos Rivera's plans to be rid of her?

The thought brought her pause. Had Pieter guessed that she had more spirit and determination that she had known herself? Was that why he had sent her—to deliberately enrage Rivera? Had Pieter decided the man needed a little healthy antagonism to pull him out of a destructive self-absorption? But he had obviously known that Rivera would have never agreed to having a woman come. Why? It was all too much of a puzzle for her tired brain to think out.

And she must remember to call him Marcos now. She had thrown down the gauntlet and it wouldn't do to show any weakness, even though it seemed like a terrible presumption to call him by his first name.

Marcos. In that first moment of meeting, he had destroyed all her childish fantasies of him. The reality was nothing like she remembered, nor did it fit the public image created by the gossip columns.

Well, she was here now, and here she would stay. Nothing he could dream up was going to drive her away!

Chapter Three

$\mathcal{T}$ hree days later Alex lay stretched out on a towel on the beach, turning frequently to get a nice, even tan. The water had felt wonderful this afternoon, for it was a particularly hot and sticky day. She had never swum in ocean like this before. The first day she had tried to walk out beyond her depth, but after going nearly a hundred yards, she found that the water still came only to her waist. As the tide turned she discovered bodysurfing—swimming out, then riding back on the huge breakers, some ten and twelve feet high, pounding their way toward shore. She was becoming quite adept at timing her leap just right so that she was able to catch the wave just before it broke.

The hottest part of the afternoons she had spent exploring the house, and to her disappointment had found little of interest. Many of the doors were kept locked, making it impossible to enter either the north or south wings of the house.

Of Marcos she had seen practically nothing. The only time they met was for dinner—which, she was amused to note, now had a more varied menu. He greeted her each evening with a formal politeness and then proceeded to ignore her studiously as he ate. During the past two nights, she had managed to maintain a one-sided conversation, but her supply of idle chatter was fast running out. His silence made her uneasy, for every now and then she would glance at him and surprise on his face a look of such anger and bitterness that it chilled her to the bone. Her one consolation was that she was as certain as she could be in the circumstances that his haunted look was not caused by her presence. No, she thought ruefully, she had not aroused his hatred, only his indifference.

Lazily she turned over on her stomach and propped her hands under her chin to look ahead at the moldering mansion turned mellow yellow by the late-afternoon glow. Idly she watched a bird in flight as it soared above the roof of the house and into the trees beyond. Suddenly her eyes focused on a single spot in the back wall. She looked for a moment and then sat up. How stupid of her not to have noticed before! But then it was in a Poe story or perhaps a Sherlock Holmes novel that the detective had said that one didn't notice the commonplace, the ordinary that was right under one's nose.

What had caught Alex's attention were power lines running through the trees to an electrical box on the outside wall of the south wing of the house. And they appeared to be in perfectly good order! The trees had been carefully cut away from them where they entered the woods. Now she thought about it, she had seen no signs of a kitchen in the center wing, nor was there any indication that any real living took place except in the drawing room. She was now willing to bet that, though the rest of the house had been closed up, the south section had been modernized and made quite livable.

For a moment she fumed at Marcos's deception. All the evenings she had spent trying to read herself to sleep by the light of a kerosene lantern while he was enjoying the convenience of electric lights. And that bathroom!

Angry color rose in Alex's cheeks. She had been perfectly willing to endure the hardships of the house before, but her sense of justice rebelled at the idea of his living in comparative comfort while she struggled to keep clean with nothing but a few pitchers of water hauled up to her room by a resentful Tomás. And no wonder he was resentful!

She bit her lip in thought. What should she do? Confront Marcos with her suspicions? No, she decided. She would try a little breaking and entering first to make certain her suspicions were correct.

Her suit was dry enough now for her to pull

on her slacks and blouse. She wiped the sand off her feet and slipped into her sandals.

Nonchalantly she crossed the beach to the patio, but once close to the house she slipped into the bushes and discovered a path through the undergrowth. Keeping low, she made her way around the end of the south wing to the far side. Luck was with her. Her trespassing would involve entering but not breaking, for a large set of windows stood open and the drapes were pulled back to let in a breeze. Carefully she hoisted herself over the low sill and into the room. At last she had found the music room where Marcos worked, she thought smugly.

A grand piano dominated the space at one end of the room. Several sheets of scored paper were on the stand, while a table nearby held a collection of music books and lined paper. The room itself was clean and beautifully kept. The walls were wood-paneled and the furniture was old but comfortable and in excellent repair. A heavy woven carpet covered the floor. Two crystal chandeliers hung from the fourteen-foot-high ceiling, and a standing lamp was placed near the piano. A huge stone fireplace was set in the wall between the windows.

Alex went to the piano first and with a quick flick of the switch turned on the lamp. It worked. Just as quickly she turned it off again.

She could hear the murmur of voices

through the open double doors coming from down the hall. Good! Marcos and Tomás were together.

Quietly she moved down the broad hallway to the open door of what appeared to be the study. Through a crack she could see built-in bookshelves lining one entire wall. The murmur was now distinct, but she caught her own name—and blushed. Wasn't the old saying that eavesdroppers never hear any good of themselves? Well, she was left no illusions about herself. Stubborn and pushy were two of Marcos's milder adjectives. Not wishing to eavesdrop further, she walked casually into the room after a perfunctory knock on the door.

"Hello," she said cheerfully to the two nonplussed men. "I finished reading the books I brought with me and wondered if you would mind lending me something else."

"What the—!" Marcos began as he leaped to his feet.

"This is a cozy room," she continued as though he hadn't spoken. "I can see why you spend so much of your time here."

"How did you get in here?" His expression was thunderous, but Alex refused to be cowed.

"Come on, Marcos. You couldn't expect me to keep up this charade forever! We have work to do." She forced a smile to her lips and addressed the astounded pair in Spanish. "And don't blame Tomás. He has faithfully kept the doors locked. I came in the window of the music room."

"Leave us, Tomás!" Marcos snapped, and quickly the man effaced himself.

"Quite correct not to quarrel in front of the servants," Alex observed dryly. "You know, Marcos, you really are a throwback to the Golden Age of Spain, aren't you."

"What I am has nothing to do with you, *Miss Stephens!*"

"Oh, call me Alex, please." She smiled innocently, a dimple flashing in her cheek. "After all, I've been calling you Marcos for three days now." Quickly she changed the subject and moved farther into the room. "What a lovely place this is."

"All right, *Alex,*" he said nastily. "You've won. You don't need to rub it in." Subsiding into his chair, he watched her with a smoldering gaze as she strolled casually around, examining the room.

Alex was suddenly horrified at her own impertinence, and she fervently hoped that Marcos couldn't see her heart pounding beneath her blouse. Marcos Rivera was not a man to be trifled with, to be teased and mocked, and she had a nervous feeling that she was like a child playing with fire. But his treatment of her, his attitude, had stirred something before unknown in her. Perhaps it was a latent feminine pique that objected to the way he seemed able to ignore her at will when she was so very aware of him.

His continued silence was making her more and more nervous, but for the life of her she couldn't think of anything to say to lighten the ominous mood as he watched her through those half-closed eyes that concealed so much of what he was thinking.

"You are a very clever woman," he offered at last. "Very resourceful." His eyes roamed slowly up her slender body to the swell of her breasts, to her face flushed now under his scrutiny, to her hair curling tightly around her head in wild disorder. "Yes," he continued thoughtfully as he rose and pulled the bell that hung behind the desk, "it is just possible that you might have . . . your uses."

"You—you mean we can begin working on your music?" she asked hesitantly, not at all sure that was what he meant.

"Mmm, we'll see," he murmured noncommittally. "Ah, Tomás," he addressed the man as he entered, "see that Miss Stephens's things are brought down."

"She's leaving!" The servant sighed with satisfaction.

"No, no. Miss Stephens prefers to stay awhile. Put her in the room we had originally prepared."

The room next to his own! Alex had a highly retentive memory. "Oh, please! Don't bother!" she interjected quickly. "I'm quite content where I am, honestly. If there is just another bathroom somewhere I could use . . . ?"

"I wouldn't dream of leaving you in such discomfort," Marcos replied silkily. "You were right. The little charade is over, and we've both enjoyed the joke, I think. Now it is time to turn our thoughts to . . . more serious matters."

His voice was low and purring now and vaguely accented, as it became, she had noticed, when he was emotional. Suddenly he looked very foreign to her—pure Castilian— with his tight black pants and his white silk shirt unbuttoned nearly to his waist so that she could see the fine mat of dark hair on his chest that curled around his silver chain and medallion. His shoulders were broad, but his waist and hips were narrow and supple. In some previous existence he could have been a matador.

"Señor Rivera—" she began.

"Marcos, Alex. It must be Marcos," he said softly. His lips smiled, but the smile did not reach his eyes. "Come, I will show you over my little hideaway. Tomás will soon have your clothes transferred, and you can bathe and change for dinner. We will dress tonight, hmmm? After all, isn't our truce a cause for celebration? We'll drink champagne and toast to . . . a better understanding, a closer friendship."

As Alex stood immobile Marcos came slowly around the edge of the desk and held out his hand to her. "Come."

She had made the mistake of looking into

his eyes and was mesmerized by the expression she saw there. Her breathing became shallow, and she could feel her heart beating erratically. Slowly she dropped her gaze to his waiting hand, and hesitantly she put her own in his. As his fingers tightened around hers she felt shock waves run up her arm.

"You are so small, so fragile," he murmured. "I could almost crush you with my one good hand."

Alex had been thinking much the same thing, and involuntarily she shivered.

"But you must not be afraid of me." He laughed, seeing her nervousness. "My anger is gone. I am now prepared to be very kind."

He did not release her hand as he drew her from the room and down the hall. One after another he threw open doors for her inspection, but beyond a vague impression of warmth and luxury she saw nothing. Her brain seemed frozen. Before, the isolation of the *casa* had not bothered her. In fact, she had found the solitude very pleasant, but now she realized just how much she was cut off from civilization with this man. They were miles from town, surrounded by jungle and ocean, and she had no means of escape but her own two legs. But surely she had nothing to fear—had she?

She breathed a heavy sigh of relief when he finally left her in her new room and the door closed behind him. Tomás had been very quick. Her clothes now hung in the wardrobes and filled the heavy armoire. A full-length mirror hung on one wall, and a glimpse of her own reflection gave her new courage. Surely she had misinterpreted Marcos's meaning. She was a sight, certainly nothing to attract a man known for his taste in beautiful women. In fact, as she looked at her disheveled appearance, her confidence grew. To her own critical eyes, she looked small and insignificant, still very thin, with prominent bones and hollows in her cheeks. What had Marcos called her that first night? Five foot four of nothing.

Satisfied that she had nothing to worry about, she turned to explore the room— particularly the bathroom. The tub was a modern white porcelain, and the water from the taps ran pure and clear. Oh, what heaven to be able to take a long, leisurely bath!

After soaking away her tension, Alex chose a gold printed silk dress for dinner, as much to boost her own morale as to comply with Marcos's request. The sleeves and skirt were long and full and very modest, but the front neckline scooped to just above the full line of her breasts. She filled in what seemed to her a broad expanse of exposed flesh with a filigreed gold necklace. Her newly washed hair was easy to arrange, for the humidity brought out all its natural wave, so she had only to brush the curls away from her face into some semblance of order. The back curved under, smooth and shining, over her shoulders to just above her waist. She applied very little makeup—some mascara on her long dark lashes, a pale lip gloss, and a smattering of powder across her nose to take off the shine.

Alex laughed to herself as she turned in front of the mirror to get a better look at herself. She had never dressed like this before and felt a little foolish, like a child playing dress-up with someone else's clothes. No doubt her father would have disapproved heartily of her appearance. Poor Nikolas, she thought with a new awareness. What little fun he had had in his life. But then, who was to say what was necessary for another person's happiness? Once again she had cause to be grateful to Pieter for his wisdom.

Hesitantly she paused at the bottom of the staircase. Now, if she could just remember which room Marcos had pointed out as the dining room. As it happened, she didn't have to search far. Tomás was just coming out of the kitchen carrying a plate of hors d'oeuvres, and he guided her to a sitting room where Marcos was already waiting. Her host rose as she entered and took her hand in his.

"You look beautiful, my dear," he said huskily as his lips brushed the back of her hand. Once again she was aware of the electricity in his touch and almost snatched her hand away, lowering her eyes too quickly to catch the gleam of sardonic amusement that flickered in his own. "What would you like to drink?" he asked, crossing to the well-stocked bar against one wall.

"Just—just some fruit juice," she stammered, unsure of herself once more. She had felt confident when she was alone, but back in Marcos's disturbing presence, her courage failed her. He had dressed in a formal white dinner jacket that set off his tan complexion and smooth dark hair. The contrast of his green eyes was devastating.

The glass he handed to her looked as if it held fruit juice, but one sip told her that wasn't all it contained. "A special concoction of my own. Quite mild," he explained when he saw the question in her eyes. "Just a little tequila, lime, and passion fruit." She sipped it warily but had to admit that it tasted delicious and quite innocuous. Casually he took a seat beside her on the wide sofa. "Have you lived in Boston all your life?"

That was the first personal question he had put to her since her arrival, but she had had her answers prepared in advance. "Yes, that has been my home. I was away at school for a number of years, though." Her reply was truthful if incomplete.

"I am surprised your family would allow you to journey so far from home."

Alex was quick to catch the implied question in his words. "I—I have no family. My father died a short time ago. So I'm on my own. Except for P—Mr. van Loos, of course. He—he's been very helpful."

"Yes, of course. Pieter." The look he gave her was full of speculation, but she met it squarely. "It isn't often that he allows his emotions to overcome his professional judgment."

"And you think that's the case with me?" She bristled.

"I didn't say that, now, did I?" he returned mildly, but she knew what he was thinking. "You are very young to take on a commission like this."

"I told you, I'm twenty-four and have had a good deal of experience!"

"I sincerely hope so! You are a very attractive woman." His heavy lids didn't quite conceal the bright gleam in his eyes, and his smile was more a leer.

"I was speaking of professional experience," she replied stiffly, the color blazing in her face.

"Oh, yes. How silly of me," he mocked her. "You really must play for me sometime."

She was prevented a scathing retort by Tomás's arrival on the scene announcing dinner, and thankfully she rose to precede the men into the adjoining dining room. This room was much different from the airless drawing room where they had eaten before. Alex's heart beat heavily as Marcos seated her at the table. The sweet fragrance of the flowers on the table, the gleam of old china and crystal, the flickering light of the candles, Marcos's assiduous attention—all invested the meal with the intimacy of a tête-à-tête.

Tonight Tomás had outdone himself. Avocado and crabmeat salad was followed by squab, roasted to perfection and accompanied by little new potatoes and yams. The bottle of champagne stood in an ornate silver wine bucket at Marcos's elbow, and he filled their glasses often.

For the first time Marcos aided the conversation, asking her more about herself but avoiding the subject of her music, as though he preferred not to know. Beyond mentioning that she had traveled some, Alex told him little of her life, and they passed most of the time discussing places that they had both visited. All the time he watched her with eyes turned warm by the candlelight.

"How is it that a beautiful woman like yourself has reached the ripe old age of twenty-four without marrying?" he asked at last as he peeled a mango for her.

"I—I haven't had time for anything but my music," she answered hesitantly.

"You must have been devoted," he said cynically. "You have such an . . . untouched air about you. But surely there have been many men in your life."

"I'm afraid not," she replied coolly.

His gaze assessed her qualities, and he appeared to like what he saw very much. "I can't believe you are really as cold as you sound. Your eyes are such a soft brown. It will be interesting to see them warm with fire. And your mouth." His eyes lingered on her soft, quivering lips. "It is just made to be kissed." Abruptly he rose to his feet and moved around to pull out her chair. "Come, let us go back into the sitting room where . . . we can be more comfortable."

Everything about the man spelled danger, and Alex's impulse was to run, to lock herself in her room and never come out. She had never been so frightened in her life. But it was her own reactions that frightened her as much as Marcos's obvious advances. Her heart was fluttering and her pulse racing. His smooth, low voice was like the caress of velvet, sending tingles down her spine. What had come over him? she wondered wildly. Where was her hostile antagonist of the previous days?

The thought gave her pause, and she frowned. What had made him change his attitude toward her? Certainly nothing she had said or done. She glanced at him quickly and caught the cold, calculating look in his eyes. Nothing the least bit loverlike in that cool green stare. Then what game was he playing now?

Of course! And she could have laughed in relief. How stupid of her not to have guessed before! Like a ninny she had fallen for his latest gambit.

Marcos wasn't interested in her as a woman. His purpose was the same as ever—to get her out of his house—and this was just another scheme. Her discovery this afternoon had put an end to his hope that neglect and the uncomfortable living conditions would drive her away, so he was trying a new tactic.

If dirt and bugs wouldn't get rid of her, he would take a hand in her departure himself. Did she appear so easily frightened by his attentions? Very probably, she thought ruefully. Just how far was he prepared to go with his pretended seduction? she wondered, and her pulse raced alarmingly at the thought.

He was walking close beside her, so that his arm brushed against her as they moved and sent chills up her spine. Did he guess that she had never really been kissed?

Once inside the sitting room, Marcos closed the door behind him and leaned negligently against it as Alex made her way quickly to the sofa. Her mind was racing, unsure yet just how she was going to handle the situation. Slowly he crossed to her and sat beside her, his arm stretched along the back of the sofa.

"You are very quiet, *chiquita*," he murmured softly. "What thoughts are going through that lovely little head of yours?" Gently he took a lock of her hair and wound it around his supple fingers.

"Oh, I was just thinking how much I've enjoyed being here," she answered lightly, refusing to look in his direction.

"I was very foolish not to bring you to my little nest in the beginning. Just my stubbornness. You understand. Am I forgiven?" He tugged slightly on the hair, forcing her to turn her head toward him. "Look at me, Alex. Let me read in your eyes what you are thinking."

He was closer than she realized, and as she turned, her leg brushed against his thigh. His eyes were not cold now, but a rich, glowing jade that made her catch her breath. His hand moved under her hair to her neck, and he gently caressed the soft skin with his thumb.

"You are very beautiful," he breathed as he slowly pulled her head closer until her lips were only inches from his. Alex knew she ought to pull away, but she was caught in the deep pools of his eyes. For the first time in her life she felt like a woman with a woman's desires, and the temptation of Eve was upon her. Just once she wanted to feel those hard, firm lips on her own.

As it happened, Marcos gave her no time to either repulse or assist him. His hand pulled her forward as his lips came down on hers in a kiss that took her breath away. There was nothing gentle or patient in that kiss. It took no account of her inexperience but demanded a response from her, forcing her lips apart and making her senses swim. At first she held herself rigid, but as the kiss deepened she felt too weak to resist the pressure of his arm as it enclosed her, and she fell against his hard, muscular chest.

Now his hand slipped down her back, seeking out the bare skin exposed by the cut of her gown, and she was caught between the caressing warmth of his hand and the hot insistence of his mouth.

On and on the ruthless kiss went, arousing in her feelings she had never dreamed she possessed. Her body began to tremble in his hold. One arm moved to his shoulder and then around the strong column of his neck. As he felt her answering response the kiss began to change in nature. His mouth became more gentle, more subtle. His lips now moved on hers with a sensual ease, inviting where they had at first demanded, coaxing submission when before they had plundered. A thrill of pleasure rippled through her as he beguiled her into surrender, and she returned his embrace with her mouth soft and yielding.

Finally, on a shuddering sigh, he released her, but she kept her eyes closed and continued to lean weakly against his broad shoulder. With the back of his injured hand he reached up and brushed the heavy waves of hair from her forehead so he could look down into her face. Slowly she opened her eyes and met his searching gaze. Whatever his intentions had been, it gave her back her pride to see that he, too, had been moved by the kiss. His mouth was taut, and faint beads of perspiration were appearing on his upper lip.

A smile of singular sweetness curved the lovely line of her mouth as she said softly,

"Thank you, Marcos. That was my first kiss, and I appreciate your making it a memorable experience."

She had no way of knowing what reaction he had expected, but that obviously hadn't been it. He was both surprised and incredulous.

"Your first kiss!"

"Yes, but you probably suspected from the beginning that I had had little experience with men. Wasn't that what you counted on? I know you aren't really . . . well, interested in me. This was just a new plot to scare me away." She laughed self-consciously. "I can't help but wonder, though, what you would have done if I weren't the kind of woman you thought me to be and I had taken you seriously."

Just for a moment his lips tightened and the hard look returned to his eyes. "What makes you think I'm not serious?"

"Oh, common sense," she replied thoughtfully. "I may be naïve, but I'm not stupid, you know. For three days you hardly notice I exist, and then—bingo! The reversal was too quick." She smiled mischievously. "And, too, your women have always been the beautiful, sophisticated sort. I'm just not in their class. But if it's any consolation," she hurried on as he stiffened. "I admit that you had me running scared for a while."

Abruptly he removed his arm from behind

her and reached to the table for a cigarette. "You seem to know a great deal about me," he said dryly.

"I've followed your career for years. Your private life hasn't exactly been kept secret," she drawled. "And you won't remember, but Pieter introduced us once—oh, years ago, in London after a concert. Rachmaninoff. You were wonderful," she added sincerely.

"We have met before?" he asked, startled. "I don't remember."

"Of course you wouldn't. There must have been a hundred people at the party, and I was only a schoolgirl."

His brow knit into a frown as he thought back. "London. After a Rachmaninoff concert. There was someone with Pieter," he said slowly. "I remember."

Alex suddenly realized that she was treading on dangerous ground. She didn't want him to remember! Given too much information, he was likely to put two and two together and come up with Alexandra Stephanos, and she was not prepared to assume her old identity. In fact, these days had seen her renaissance. As far as she was concerned, Alexandra Stephanos was gone for the duration. She had no desire to go back to the life of that dull, repressed, dedicated woman. She was Alex Stephens now, and Alex she would stay.

"How well do you really know Pieter?" he asked abruptly, breaking into her thoughts.

"I've known him since I was a baby," she answered truthfully—no harm in that. "He—he was a friend of my family."

"How well do you play?"

"Pieter has confidence in my ability," she responded carefully.

"And yet he allows you to earn your living in a nightclub! Has he never considered managing your career?"

"We—we've talked about it, but he felt I wasn't ready. That—that was one of the reasons he sent me here, I think."

"And yet he thinks you have enough experience to be of use to me!"

The expression on his face wasn't encouraging, but this was the moment to take the plunge. Reaching out cautiously, she touched the back of his injured hand.

"Marcos," she said gently, "I know you don't want me here. I know that you are only honoring your promise to Pieter. But you have to see that I made him a similar promise. I promised to stay—no matter what. I—I sincerely believe I can be of help to you, but we'll make a bargain. Listen to me play. Let me work with you for , . . oh, say a couple of weeks. And then, if you honestly feel that you are wasting your time, I'll go back to Pieter and make him understand. I'll make him release you from your promise—but only if you will give me a fair chance."

He sat very still as he looked down into her earnest young face. She read all the doubts and reservations in the grim line of his lips, and in his eyes was something more. It could have been pain; she wasn't sure.

"All right," he said at last. "We'll give it a fair trial." Restlessly he ran his fingers through his hair. "I need to work. I have been able to accomplish a little in the past few weeks since I was released from the hospital, but it has been slow going."

"There—there is no hope at all that you'll recover the use of your hand?" she asked hesitantly.

"None! The last operation was meant to accomplish as much as is possible. If it was successful, I will have the use of all but two fingers, but that is little consolation!" His mouth set in bitter lines. "But we will talk of it no more!"

"When do we begin?" she asked quickly, wanting to take his mind off his hand.

"Tomorrow. Meet me in the music room after breakfast." A wry smile twisted his lips. "I believe you know already where that is."

"Tomorrow morning, then." She rose to her feet, but he caught her hand and looked at her expressive mouth, the copper highlights in her dark hair, her warm, compassionate eyes. "You don't want to stay a little longer?" His eyes were searching, his smile mocking. "We could always pick up where we left off."

"Thank you, but I'll pass this time." She laughed, but the color flooded her face. "After all, my education has increased a hundred percent tonight. I think that's probably enough for one evening!"

"Strictly grammar-school knowledge, Alex," he drawled. "I'd be delighted to take you on into higher education."

"No, thanks, Marcos!"

"Another time, perhaps." And the grip on her hand tightened.

"Thanks again, but I think I'll stick to book learning."

"That's no substitute for practical application."

"I'm afraid you're far too expert to be satisfied with a novice like me," she said lightly, trying to pull her hand free. "And didn't I read that a lovely dark-eyed señorita held a special place in your affections?"

She had only meant to tease, but whatever she had said had wiped the smile from his lips and brought the fierce frown back to his face. He dropped her hand as though her touch burned him, and Alex would have given anything to have taken back her words. For just a few moments he had been his old, charming self, but once again she had reawakened his hostility and antagonism.

"Good night, then," he said curtly. "I'll see you in the morning."

As Alex undressed for bed she went back over the strange evening. She didn't allow her thoughts to dwell long on the kiss—its memory was still too disturbing. Instead she remembered his reaction to her last comment.

Her reference to his lady friend had struck a nerve, and it gave her some clue to his present animosity toward women. Obviously, whoever the woman was, she had hurt him deeply and left him bitter. Had she been unwilling to stand by after his hand was injured and he had been forced to give up his career? Or perhaps it had been a quarrel of another kind.

She shrugged philosophically. She would probably never know, but at least she could take some comfort in the knowledge that he hadn't taken a dislike to her personally, that his hostility was directed at her sex in general.

Hostility? The memory of his kiss and the subsequent exchange of words intruded on her thoughts. Whatever the emotion was that had resulted from that kiss, it hadn't been hostility! He might despise women, but he obviously hadn't totally rejected the need for them in his life, and that awareness made her nerves quiver.

She had the disquieting premonition that if she had any sense at all, she would leave San Blas before she found herself caught up in the loves and hates of this enigmatic man. His complexities were beyond her simple knowledge of men. But she couldn't bring herself to leave now, and honesty compelled her to admit that it had less to do with her promise to Pieter than something within herself.

She had met the first hurdles and cleared them. Tomorrow Marcos would listen to her play. Yes. It must be her pride that kept her there, she concluded as she turned out the light. She wanted to prove herself to him. But nagging doubts followed her into sleep.

Chapter Four

$\mathscr{F}$or the first time Marcos joined Alex for breakfast, and though it was still early, she had the feeling he had been up for hours. His eyes were bright and alert, and he had the smell of the sea about him.

While Alex dawdled over orange juice, a roll, and cinnamon-spiced Mexican chocolate Marcos put away a substantial meal. He said little, and Alex, used to her father's silent, irritable mornings, kept quiet and let him eat in peace, wanting to do nothing that would upset the tenuous truce between them.

Finally he rose and tossed his napkin on the table. "Fifteen minutes, in the music room," he said tersely and left.

Alex took that time to calm her quivering nerves. Her stomach was in knots. She had never been more anxious, not even before an important concert. The thought of playing for a critical audience of one was far more terrifying than performing for an impersonal, crowd-filled hall—especially when that audience was Marcos Rivera.

He was waiting for her when she finally pushed open the doors to the music room. His grim expression did not augur well for the success of the venture, but Alex straightened her shoulders and entered with all the confidence she could summon.

"Sit down, sit down!" he commanded as she hovered by the bench. "What do you want to play? There are books on the table beside you."

Alex hesitated. "Would—would you mind if I warm up a little first? I haven't touched a piano for nearly a week."

"All right." He sighed in resignation, checked his watch, and, with more consideration than she had expected, moved to the door. "I'll give you ten minutes alone. But then I'll be back." And to her sensitive ears his words sounded like a threat.

As the door closed behind him she ran her fingers experimentally over the keys. The piano had a beautiful tone and was obviously kept in perfect tune. The minute her fingers formed the first chord, all her nervousness went from her. This was her life, her joy, and she gave herself up to the music. At random she began a Bach prelude, slow and moving. From there she moved on to Mozart, and finally to Chopin.

Oh, how she had missed the comfort of playing this last week! And she was so caught up in the lovely, lilting melodies that she didn't even hear Marcos return. From the doorway he watched her for a moment and then moved silently across the carpet to sit in a high-backed easy chair.

On and on she played, and the time slipped away from her. It wasn't until she had been at the piano for nearly forty-five minutes that she stopped abruptly in the middle of a Chopin nocturne and looked toward the door. Where had Marcos gone?

"Finish it!" he snapped from his chair across the room—and she jumped.

"I—I didn't hear you come in," she offered lamely.

"Finish it!" he repeated and leaned his head back against the chair and closed his eyes.

Alex went back a few measures to where the theme began again and played the music through to the end. As the final notes died away she took her hands from the keys and folded them quietly in her lap, her eyes on Marcos's impassive face.

"Where were you trained?" he asked sharply as he rose and came to her side, and Alex named her teachers both at home and abroad.

"How long have you been playing?" he inquired more gently.

"All my life," she answered simply.

"And with a gift like that, Pieter allows you to play in a nightclub? It is a terrible waste!"

Alex's heart was filled with joy. No praise had ever meant more to her, and she would have explained her lie about the nightclub, but Marcos was hurrying on, a suppressed excitement about him. "Today I will give you the first movement of my suite. Work on it. Acquire a feel for what I am trying to accomplish. Tonight you can play it for me."

He turned to the table behind him and shuffled through the papers there, at last coming up with the manuscript he looked for and placing it on the piano. "If you have any questions, I'll be in my study."

Alex waited until he had gone to leaf through the pages. This first movement he had called simply *Allegro*. He had obviously written the music rapidly, but the notes were clear and his markings explicit. Tentatively she began the opening chords, but as the music swelled from under her fingers she played with more assurance. The tone was full and rich—substantial. The melody was slightly disturbing, the harmony complex, and the dissonant counterpoint in the left hand gave the work a contemporary flavor that intrigued her.

All morning she worked, perfecting the dynamics here, a trill there, and as the clock in the room struck noon she relaxed back, exhausted. If she was any judge—and she prided herself that she was—this music was brilliant. Pieter had certainly been right about Marcos's ability as a composer. How much more of the work had he completed? She was now very eager to play the rest, and for a minute she was tempted to search through

the pile of papers and find the next movement. Prudence, however, stopped her. She
must not push Marcos too fast. Let him take
her along at his own speed. Tonight, if he was
satisfied, she would ask for more, and the
evening couldn't come fast enough to suit her.

After a quick, solitary lunch, she whiled
away the afternoon hours on the beach and
returned to her rooms to soak the salt from
her skin in a long, cool bath. That night she
dressed for dinner with the same care she
would have given her preparations for a concert. Not black crêpe, however—she had left
those somber dresses hanging in her closet in
Boston. She chose instead a short, cream-
colored silk designed along Grecian lines—
sleeveless and bloused at the waist. The soft
color set off her newly acquired tan to perfection. The dress was simple but cut superbly so
that it moved and flowed around her legs as
she walked.

Instead of the severe chignon, she opted for
a loose bun on the top of her head that would
keep her hair out of her face as she played but
was still soft and feminine. A few tendrils of
hair curled lovingly down over her ears and
onto her forehead. Tonight she applied more
eye makeup than she usually wore for casual
dress—eyeliner, mascara, and a light, lumi-
nous eye shadow that made her eyes appear
large and lustrous. Again, she applied just a
pale lip gloss and a light touch of powder. The
overall effect was intended to make her look

older and, she hoped, sophisticated. She didn't want Marcos to call her a child ever again, and especially not this evening.

He hadn't dressed formally for dinner, but he was immaculately groomed in tan slacks and an olive-green shirt, open at the neck, that emphasized the broadness of his shoulders and the color of his eyes.

As dinner was served, Alex waited for him to bring up the subject of his music, but she was to be disappointed. He carefully controlled the conversation so that while they discussed music in general, they did not discuss his work.

"I might have guessed you would play Chopin a great deal," he said at one point. "You often have that soft, dreamy look in your eye that speaks of a romantic. You probably prefer Schubert and Mendelssohn to Beethoven, say, or Haydn."

"Unfair." She laughed. "I play them all. Different music to suit different moods. I've even been known to dabble with Prokofiev and Bartók. So there!"

It wasn't until over coffee in the sitting room that Marcos asked her casually—too casually—"Have you played much of Hindemith's work?"

Alex knew the work of the contemporary German composer well, and she also knew that this was a leading question, apparently a test for her. But she didn't need time to consider her answer.

"Yes." She smiled. "I've played him enough to know that he was your inspiration in the *Allegro* movement you gave me. You've enhanced the feeling of motion in the arpeggios by using dissonance in the counterpoint, the same way he used it."

He was obviously pleased and impressed with her answer, although beyond a "Humph!" he didn't comment but continued to study her silently for a moment. At last he seemed to settle an internal struggle. "All right! Come and play for me."

That morning Alex had been very nervous, but tonight she was strangely confident. Perhaps it was because she genuinely liked his composition. What would she have done if she hadn't? Somehow she doubted that she would have had the nerve to tell him the truth.

The chandeliers were already lighted, but Marcos turned on the lamp to give her better illumination. She took her place at the piano, waited for him to take a seat, arranged the pages so that the music could be easily turned —and began.

After the first eight measures, all was forgotten but the music. Time and place slipped away. She felt caught up in the drama of the composition—the whirl and bustle of city life, traffic and people hurrying this way and that. In the middle was a dark passage, heavy with menace. Running, running—but getting nowhere. At the end came the interwoven themes, the chaos with its undercurrent of the dark and oppressive. The music did not build to a crescendo at that point; rather, there was a slowing down, a fading out, a lulling, and then the crashing chords of the ending, loud and jarring.

As Alex let her hands slip from the keys she felt totally drained, not just from the physical effort of executing the highly technical arrangement but also from the emotional pull she felt in every note. Slowly she came back from her never-never land, back to the present, and her eyes focused once again and picked out Marcos sitting rigid in his chair, not saying a word.

"It's the city, isn't it, Marcos?" she asked softly. "Where?"

"Where do you think it is?" His voice was low and strained.

"It could be any big city—London, New York, Tokyo, Paris," she answered hesitantly. Had she offended him?

Suddenly he dropped his head in his hands as she watched in horrified silence. She didn't dare to move a muscle. When he raised his head a moment later, it seemed as though he had aged ten years before her eyes. His face looked ravaged, the lines around his nose and mouth more pronounced than she had ever seen them, his green eyes like glowing jewels in dark, sunken pits. His whole expression was haunted.

"Are—are you all right?" she felt compelled to ask.

"No! No, I am not all right!"

"The work. It—it's brilliant, Marcos. I know it is. I feel it!"

"And I will never be able to play it for myself! Never! That music is a part of me, a part of my immortal soul! And I will never be able to play it again, not as you did just now!"

Over the past few days Alex had often witnessed the bitterness in him, but not this black rage, this hopeless despair that tore at her heart. She wanted to go to him, to hold him, comfort him, until it passed. Only another artist, to whom music meant life, could understand the terrible, soul-destroying loss Marcos Rivera had suffered. It had little to do with the loss of his career. It was the terrible inability to satisfy needs and longings in the heart and soul that demanded expression.

Oh, if there were only some way she could help him! Could help lift this terrible burden from him! She would willingly dedicate half her life to that end.

What she was feeling must have shown in her face, for suddenly he flew at her, his face contorted into a savage mask of hatred. "Get out!" he snarled. "I don't need you, your pity! Not a woman! Twisted, twisted and inhuman. Souls like the devil himself. Selfish, deceitful, lying—"

Alex didn't wait to hear any more. Marcos stood over her like an avenging angel, and she quickly slipped past him and out the door, closing it behind her. In her haste she nearly stumbled into Tomás standing in the hallway. His face was dark and impassive, but his eyes were warm with sympathy—not for her, she was sure, but for his master.

"Señorita Stephens," he said when she would have brushed by him.

"Y-yes, Tomás?" She hesitated.

"He doesn't mean all he says. He'll be all right tomorrow. You'll see. Stay here. He needs you. You are not like that other one. You understand. You can help him where no one else can."

For the first time since that awful scene, Alex felt as though she could breathe again. She expelled her breath on a long, pent-up sigh and looked up into the man's anxious eyes.

"It's all right, Tomás. I do understand, and I won't go now."

"He is like a wounded lion, but it is not right for him to hide himself and bear his hurts alone. He needs to work, to feel purpose again."

"I know, Tomás, and I wouldn't dream of leaving him, not as long as I can help him." And she smiled reassuringly.

"You are not offended?" he asked curiously.

"No." She smiled ruefully. "I'm not offended. I'm afraid that I'm used to what's called artistic temperament." But she knew that what Marcos was feeling was more, oh, so much more, than that.

A beautiful smile broke over the old man's

lined face. "You are a nice person. For a woman, that is," he amended. But, considering the source, Alex took this as high praise indeed, and she went to her room with a lighter heart than she would have thought possible. If the person closest to Marcos felt everything would turn out all right, surely she had to hope, too.

Still, Alex slept badly. She couldn't erase the sight of Marcos's tortured face from her thoughts, and when she awoke from her troubled sleep with the first light of dawn, she decided to wash away some of her cares in the warm sea. She stayed out longer than she had intended, but it was still early when she slipped in the patio door of the sitting room. The sound of Marcos's voice stopped her at the entrance.

"Tomás!" he bellowed down the hall, and she heard the soft sound of the servant's step on the parquet floor.

"Señor?"

"Where is she? I looked in her room, and she's gone! Did you take her into town?"

He sounded so angry and frustrated that Alex stepped quickly from the room before Tomás could reply. "Here I am, Marcos," she said lightly. "Did you want me? I got up early so I could go swimming."

Marcos bit his lip to hold back a retort, glared at her with steely green eyes, and turned on his heel and stormed down the hall.

"You see," Tomás said. "He's fine this morning, just like I said."

Alex grimaced. If this behavior was "fine," it didn't bode well for the morning. But Marcos's treatment of her didn't bother her unduly, nor did she expect an apology from him. He didn't strike her as the type to admit being at fault. She was surprised, therefore, when he joined her at the breakfast table later and the first words he spoke were words of regret.

"I beg your pardon, Alex," he said curtly. "I—I wasn't myself last night. It is just that sometimes I . . . I—"

"You don't have to say any more, Marcos." Her voice was gentle, her eyes soft with compassion. His face was pale under his bronze skin, and there were still dark circles under his eyes as though he, too, had slept badly.

"Does that mean you'll stay?" he asked stiffly.

"Of course! Don't you know by now that I'm not so easily frightened away?" She laughed self-consciously and casually picked up a roll and spread it with thick homemade butter. "It probably does you good to go on a rampage now and then," she added practically. "Much more healthy than keeping it all bottled up inside."

She looked up and caught his eye, and the expression in his penetrating gaze made her pale and drop her own eyes to her hands, which were unaccountably trembling. He seemed to be examining her face feature by feature, as though she were a strange specimen he had unearthed from under a rock. She withstood his scrutiny as long as she could, but it was making it impossible for her to eat, and finally she said tartly, "Do I have dirt on my nose or something?"

"Hmmm?" he murmured, and then, surprisingly, he smiled. "Oh, no! Your nose is just fine. It turns up on the end, you know, so that you look just a little bit haughty when you tilt your chin in that aggressive way."

He was laughing at her! And she relaxed, her composure restored by his return to good humor.

"Will—will you tell me more about your suite?" she asked diffidently, wanting to take advantage of the mood while it lasted.

"I think you know a lot of what I was trying to do. You said it yourself—the city. Variations of nighttime: the frantic chaos, the night workers, the lovers, the false gaiety of light, music, aimless movement, and then dawn— the beginning of a new day. Five movements in all."

"And you've finished—?"

"Most of the first three. I had that done when . . . when I had my accident." He stopped and ran his hand through his hair. The helpless anger warred with control, and fortunately control won. "Before, I composed at the piano," he continued after a moment.

"Now I must hear the notes in my head and play first one hand and then the other. Never to be able to play the two together—"

"Will you let me play the other two movements now?" Alex interjected quickly. "And then we can talk about the best way of working together."

As he had done the day before, he left her alone to work on the manuscript, and Alex found her admiration of him growing. The form and style of each was distinct and different, and yet each complemented the other.

The first few times through, Alex worked for a technical accuracy. She didn't want to play so much as one note wrong or vary the rhythm and dynamics from what was written by a hairsbreadth. It was very intimidating to know that the composer would be listening intently to every nuance of sound. Once she was satisfied with the mechanics, she worked on the emotions portrayed, but after Marcos's explanation of his intention, that was the easiest part of all.

Just before noon he returned, and as she began to play she uttered a silent prayer that today her playing wouldn't bring a repetition of last night's disaster. To her great relief, it didn't. She took only a slight pause between the movements and then played through to the end. Marcos was silent for a long while after she had finished, but his expression was more thoughtful than disturbed.

"I am not entirely happy with the *coda* of

the second movement," he said slowly, "but I think we'll leave it for now and come back to it later. Take a break, and we'll work after lunch."

The next few days established the pattern. Marcos worked by himself in the mornings while Alex swam or read or occasionally drove into town with Tomás to get supplies. Then after lunch they worked through what he had written. Some days he accomplished more than others, and working with him was a pleasure. On days when he struggled and came up with nothing that satisfied him, he seemed bent on making Alex share his frustration.

"Staccato! Staccato! The arpeggio must be staccato!" And he pushed her aside to demonstrate the passage one-handed.

"You don't have it marked," she replied calmly as she put the dots above the notes.

"Okay, again! And do it right this time!"

At times like this he reminded her strongly of her father, but, unlike Nikolas Stephanos, when the work went well he was unstinting in his praise of her.

"How a musician of your limited professional experience can play with such confidence, such passion, I cannot understand," he said one day. "I have known concert pianists who have been playing for years who don't have your assurance."

These moments her deceit troubled her conscience. But she had discovered in herself a latent streak of stubbornness. Her success in the past had been made possible by her father's name. She wanted to earn Marcos's respect this time on her own merits. Devoutly she prayed that he would never discover her deception, but unless Pieter told him, there was no reason why he should. She was beginning to doubt that she would ever resume her professional name and return to the world she had left. This taste of freedom had been intoxicating, and her satisfaction with the work she was doing far excelled any concert work. And there were the evenings—the best of all.

Two days after she and Marcos began their collaboration, they sat in the dining room over coffee in a companionable silence. She was growing used to his various moods and had learned when he wanted conversation to distract him from his unhappy thoughts and when he preferred quiet.

"Would you play for me this evening?" he asked abruptly.

At first she thought he meant he wanted to work, but he quickly hurried on. "I mean just for pleasure, anything you would like—if you aren't too fatigued, that is."

From then on, every evening they would retire to the music room, and Marcos would sit in his favorite chair, sipping a brandy, while Alex played. His taste, like hers, was eclectic, and from her vast repertoire she would choose a varied program. As though she were performing a concert, she thought with some amusement. Every now and then he would make a request, and if she didn't have the particular selection committed to memory, he would have the music at hand.

Never had Alex enjoyed playing more. As appreciative as audiences were on the concert tours, as Pieter had noted, she always felt a detachment. Playing for Marcos was different. He was both appreciative and educated, and she would feel his presence, his encouragement, his deep love of music that equaled her own. Every now and then he would interrupt her with a suggestion about her playing—advising here, coaching there.

"Do you feel like Liszt tonight?" he asked one evening a couple of weeks into her stay. He was reclining in his favorite chair, looking very relaxed and pleased with the world. As well he might, Alex thought warmly. Today they had completed over half of the fourth movement.

"That's fine," she replied agreeably. "Anything special?"

"No. You choose," he murmured lazily, closing his eyes.

She began with *Will-o'-the-Wisp*, an étude that demanded the most of her fingering dexterity and light touch. Without pause she went from that to a rhapsody. The gay, joyous music exactly suited her mood that evening. She finished the piece with a flourish and turned to Marcos. "What next?"

In answer he rose and searched through a pile of music on his desk. "Try this," he said, placing several sheets of manuscript on the piano.

She recognized it immediately as one of his own compositions, though she had never seen it before. As he returned to his place, she glanced through it quickly and then began.

It, too, was a rhapsody. The influence of his Latin heritage was apparent in both the themes and the rhythm. It was an epic of Mexican nationalism, a celebration of his native land. Written for a true piano virtuoso, the massive chords, broken right-hand arpeggios, and constant ornamentation tried her almost to the limit of her ability. But she was both moved and excited by the work.

"Oh, Marcos, that's wonderful!" she cried as she finished. "Do you have a name for it?"

"I call it *Mexican Rhapsody*, what else?"

"You haven't introduced it yet?"

"No," he said curtly. "I had planned—" His upraised hand and his shrug were eloquent. "Not many pianists could play it. It hasn't been until the last week that I was convinced you could."

This accolade was spoken so casually that it took Alex a minute to absorb the importance of his words. The two-week trial period was over, and this was his way of telling her that she did indeed measure up to his high standards. The praise filled her with both pride and humility. A smile of sheer happiness broke over her face like morning sunshine.

"Thank you, Marcos."

The smile, however, slowly faded into a look of inquiry as he stared silently at her. "Marcos?" He seemed to be studying every minute detail of her appearance with such obvious appreciation that she felt the color creep up her neck and into her face. She was wearing a deep rose jersey dress that left her arms and shoulders bare and hugged every curve of her slim figure, emphasizing her tiny waist and the soft fullness of her breasts. "Marcos!" she said more insistently.

"Hmmm?" he murmured, unconcerned that she had caught him staring.

"Is—is something the matter?"

"I was just thinking," he drawled. "Let's take a break tomorrow. You've worked hard these last two weeks. You deserve a treat. I'll introduce you to my favorite swimming hole." The smile that accompanied his words was so boyish and just a little mischievous, that she couldn't help responding.

"Okay." She laughed. "But I would say that it's you who deserve the break."

"After breakfast, then. I'll have Tomás pack a lunch."

Alex slowly rose to her feet, for some reason reluctant to leave, even though she had obviously been dismissed. "Good night, then. I'll see you in the morning."

She had paused beside his chair, and unexpectedly he reached out and took her hand in his, studying the long, slim fingers, the necessarily short nails buffed to a soft pink glow.

"Such talented hands," he murmured huskily, and her heart nearly stopped beating as he raised her right hand to his lips and pressed a kiss in her palm. "Thank you, Alex."

Chapter Five

*A*lex felt unaccountably shy when she met Marcos for breakfast the next morning. She slipped quietly into her place and glanced at him long enough to note that his softened mood had survived the night and continued over to the morning. She knew that it grew out of his satisfaction with their work, and it was foolish of her to take the kiss on her hand as anything but a tribute to her diligence. Still, she felt uncomfortable with him in a new and strange way.

Perhaps, she considered objectively, it was because he was dressed much more casually today in cut-off shorts and a T-shirt that molded his broad shoulders and made her very aware of his wholly masculine form.

As usual, she waited to see if he wanted to talk during breakfast, allowing him to initiate a dialogue if he chose. Today he chose.

"We'll have Tomás drive us to the boat dock," he said. "Then he can pick us up later this afternoon."

"Where are we going?" she asked curiously.

"I'm not going to tell you." And he smiled that new, disturbing smile. "You're going to have to wait and see for yourself, but I'll wager you've never seen anything like it."

Alex wasn't to be disappointed. Midmorning they arrived at a wooden dock that jutted out into an interior canal. The motorboat tied there was small, and Marcos could easily control the tiller with one hand.

"Where are we going?" she asked once again as he headed up the canal.

"Just watch."

Within minutes they were in the heart of the jungle, and Alex let out a gasp of surprise. The canal was man-made, cut through the heart of twisted, intertwined tree roots that rose some six to eight feet above the water. The overhead branches of the trees themselves completely blocked out the sun.

"Don't be tempted to trail your hand in the water," Marcos said casually.

"Why?"

He slowed the engine until they were almost drifting and pointed to a place ahead. "Look."

Alex saw the still water move and thought for a minute that it was fish. Then she recognized her mistake and swallowed to suppress the cry that rose in her throat. Alligators!

They were small compared to those she had seen in movies, only about three or four feet long, but as one raised its head out of the water she saw that it could quite effectively remove a hand up to the wrist.

A half hour more brought them to another boat mooring. "We walk from here," Marcos explained, tossing the rope onto the dock. "Wait till I get this tied up, and then I'll help you out."

Once the boat was secured, she handed him the food and then reached up her hand. She had forgotten his power and gave a little jump as he pulled. Her momentum, coupled with the strength of his arm, made her overbalance, and she would have fallen if he hadn't caught her around the waist. As it was, she fell heavily against him, but the impact seemed to make no impression on him. He was like a rock wall, and for a moment she lay gasping against his hard chest.

She had never been this close to a man before—so close she could feel the full length of muscles in his legs, smell the masculine aroma that was a combination of good soap and sweat. The day was already hot and sticky, and the damp warmth of his arm around her penetrated the thin fabric of her blouse as he held her. Before she had time to move, she felt his muscles tense, and a second later she was free of his hold. Her heart was beating strangely, and she supposed it was from that moment of fear when she thought she was going to fall.

"You all right?" he asked, searching her face.

"Oh! Oh, yes, of course." And she laughed self-consciously. "It's a good thing you caught me, or you would have had to fish me out from the alligators!"

"Well, come on, then. Let's get going."

For some reason he seemed unusually tense. Perhaps he had hurt his hand when he caught her, she decided, and hurried to catch up with him as he strode off down the path.

They didn't speak again until just before they arrived at their destination.

"Listen," he said. "You can hear the water now."

Above the jungle noises she had grown accustomed to, she heard the sound of rushing water. "Is it a stream?"

"You'll have to wait and see."

He pushed aside a bush and allowed her to precede him through the opening. "Oh, Marcos!" she breathed. Never had she seen a sight to equal this. Before them was a waterfall, not high, probably no more than twenty feet, but wide and full, dropping into a clear pool at the bottom. Around the sides of the pool were large, flat rocks, and beyond them a profusion of plant life, trees and flowering shrubs. It looked like a jungle paradise. "Oh, Marcos," she sighed again reverently. "It's beautiful!"

"You can swim here; it's quite safe. But be careful. The water comes from underground springs and is much cooler than the ocean."

Alex had worn her suit under her clothes,

and slowly she began to unbutton her blouse, terribly conscious of Marcos's presence. He had turned his attention from the scenery to watch her with bright, interested eyes.

"Maybe—maybe I'll just look around a bit first," she said hesitantly.

"Nonsense! The water's wonderful. You won't find it unpleasant."

Thank goodness he attributed her nervousness to a fear of the water! No young woman in this day and age was worried about being seen in a swimming suit. He would think her an incredible prude.

Pretending to be looking at the water, she turned her back on him, kicked off her sandals, and slipped out of her blouse and shorts. Her suit was one piece, but it was cut high up on the sides and very low in the back. Thank goodness the top was lined! she thought.

Not daring to look to see if he was still watching, she quickly took a shallow dive into the pool. As he had said, the water was cooler than she was used to, and as she surfaced she had to pause for a moment to catch her breath. But the day itself was warm and soon the coolness felt wonderful. The water was so clear that it could hardly be considered concealing, but once submerged she felt more comfortable and even dared to look back toward the rocks where Marcos stood.

Again she had to catch her breath. He, too, had stripped, down to tan bathing trunks, and as he stood motionless, feet astride and hands on his hips, the sun playing on his golden skin made him look like a bronze statue of some ancient Greek god. His appearance, the whole setting, was so pagan that Alex felt as though she had been transported to another time, another civilization.

"Are—are you allowed to get your hand wet?" she called to break the illusion.

"No, but the sun feels good."

She watched him for a minute more until she realized that she had been openly staring, and with a quick turn she struck out for the opposite shore. For nearly an hour she swam, enjoying the fresh water after so much time in the sea. But when the sun went behind the clouds, she began to feel a little chilly, and she was faced with the realization that sooner or later she was going to have to come out of the water.

Slowly she swam toward the rock where Marcos lay stretched out on a towel. For the first little while he had watched her, but for the last half hour he had given every indication of being asleep. Perhaps, if she was very quiet, she could be out of the water and down on the rock before he noticed. She had found a toehold and was just pulling herself up, however, when he opened his eyes and looked straight into hers.

"There's another towel in the basket," he said lazily, appreciatively studying her figure in the clinging wet suit.

She had no choice but to continue her ascent from the pool under his intent gaze. She'd never felt so self-conscious in her life!

With more haste than grace she clambered up the final few feet. Grabbing the towel, she wrapped it around her shoulders and sank down on the broad rock ledge a few feet from Marcos's outstretched body. By now he had raised up and was supporting himself on one elbow, the better to see her. She started when she took a quick glance and saw the smoldering fire in his green eyes.

"Your suit will dry faster if you lie down," he suggested huskily.

Hesitantly she spread out her towel and lay down on her stomach, her head turned away from his disturbingly masculine form. A moment later she jumped as she felt his warm hand on her bare back.

"Insect repellent," he explained suavely, smoothing the lotion on her shoulders. "The mosquitoes will eat you alive if they get a taste of your soft skin."

"I—I can do that," she gasped as his fingers worked down her spine in ever narrowing circles, following the line of her suit.

"Oh? You're a contortionist, perhaps?" And he pushed her back down.

His touch was playing havoc with her nerves, and when he began on her legs, she had had all she could endure. With a jerk she turned over on her back and sat up. "Now I can reach it!"

His eyes traveled from her flushed face to

her neck, her breasts, and down the length of her body, and he frowned as he asked, "Are you sunburned, or are you blushing—all over?"

She had two choices. She could try to brazen it out, or she could tell him the truth. Being the honest girl she was, she opted for candor. "You must think I'm a fool," she mumbled, hanging her head to avoid looking at him. "It's just that . . . well, I've never been with a man dressed in nothing but a swimming suit, and no man has ever . . . well . . . touched me like that. You—you make me shy!" she finished in a rush.

For a long, tense moment he made no reply. He was so still that she forced herself to flash a quick glance at him, and what she read in his eyes made her heart drop. All the former good humor had left his face, and his eyes were dark and unfathomable as they searched her face.

"Either you are a consummate actress," he said slowly, "or you are just about the most ingenuous child I've ever met up with."

Neither description sounded particularly flattering, and she frowned, trying to read the meaning behind his words. Whatever it was, the sunshine went out of the day. The cold, shuttered look had come back into his eyes, and she sensed his mental withdrawal.

Soon after, they ate their picnic, and though he remained polite, the old cynicism was back in his smile, a faint puzzlement in his eyes.

Whatever ground she thought she had gained toward an easier friendship with him was irretrievably lost.

The next day they were back at work once again. While Alex could take pride that the work was progressing so well, at the same time she was a little dismayed at the thought that once it was done, her stay at *Casa de Rivera* would also be at an end. Marcos never referred to their outing at the waterfall, but Alex spent many sleepless hours trying to figure out what had gone wrong. She went over every word and finally had to conclude that her immaturity had annoyed him.

At least, though Marcos still had his black moods, they were of shorter duration and the periods between them were longer. During the bad times Alex took care to stay out of his way as much as possible, say little, and do nothing that would disturb him even further.

She had been in San Blas just over a month when Marcos made the surprising announcement at breakfast that they would be gone for the day. "I have an appointment in Tepic," he explained tersely, his mouth tense and grim, but Alex understood.

"Your—your hand?" she asked cautiously.

"Yes. The splints come off today. At least now I'll be able to swim again—even if it's only one-handed."

He managed so well that Alex had scarcely noticed his limitations. Had she thought about it, she realized, she would have been aware that the food Tomás prepared required little cutting, that Marcos never wore shoes that laced, or ties, or performed a hundred little tasks that would have frustrated him but which a two-handed person would take for granted.

Alex kept her face blank as she asked crisply. "What time do you want to leave?" She had learned by now that any hint of pity enraged him.

"If we leave by eleven that will give us time to have lunch before I must be at the hospital. Then this afternoon you can shop while I am occupied. If all goes well, we will stay in town this evening for dinner."

His outline for the day sounded more like orders than an invitation, but Alex wasn't deceived by his brusque manner. He was worried and anxious, and it warmed her heart to know that he desired her company at all.

"Then I'll meet you here at eleven," she replied calmly and hurried off to the momentous task of choosing an outfit to wear. She only wished the purpose of the trip could be more pleasant. What if something had gone wrong and his whole hand was still paralyzed rather than just the two fingers?

At five minutes to eleven she was waiting for him when he arrived. He had discarded his usual slacks and shirt for a blue denim suit and looked so casually elegant he took her breath away.

"Let's go," he said curtly. "Would you mind driving?"

The ride into Tepic took well over an hour because Alex had too much respect for the luxurious car to rush it over the bumpy roads. Marcos sat silent and grim beside her, and after a few tentative attempts at conversation, she gave it up. Lunch was a silent meal. His nervousness communicated itself to her, and she ate practically nothing at all. At two they arrived at the doctor's surgery in the hospital.

"You will stay with me, Alex!" Marcos ordered.

Alex found herself holding her breath as the doctor cut away the tape and gauze, carefully removed the metal brace, and finally lifted off the plastic splints. The hand underneath was pale compared with Marcos's right one, and the skin was still red in places and slightly puckered.

"Move it, señor," the doctor said gently.

Cautiously he moved his thumb and then lifted his index finger. Although the office was well air-conditioned, she could see the beads of perspiration forming on his brow from the strain.

"The third finger now," the doctor prompted.

There was a breathtaking moment of hesitation, and then the third finger moved.

"You still have no feeling in the other two fingers?"

"None," Marcos replied curtly.

"But for the rest, the operation has been successful! I will call Dr. Valdez in Mexico City. You will feel some discomfort, perhaps even pain, for the first while . . ."

The doctor continued for the next few minutes giving instructions and then called for his nurse to take the patient to physical therapy.

"You'll come back in two hours," Marcos told Alex as he turned to go.

"Yes." She frowned slightly at the tone, but then, for the first time since the episode at the pool, a full smile curved his lips and reached the depth of his eyes, and her pique melted.

"Yes," he said softly, "I think tonight we will celebrate."

The moon was full in the starlit sky that night. The café Marcos had chosen was in an interior courtyard. A balcony covered with hanging vines and flowers encircled the open space. In one corner was a dance floor where a small combo played.

Tonight Marcos was happy and relaxed in her company once again. The two damaged fingers curled slightly, but he was able now to move the others more easily, and no one would have guessed that there was anything wrong with the hand.

After the dishes had been removed, he stood and drew Alex to her feet. "Let's dance," he said softly.

The wine, the music, and the heavy scent of

flowers, combined with Marcos's return to good humor, all conspired to make her a little lightheaded. She remembered all too vividly the pleasurable feel of his hard body against hers, and she savored the moment when he put his hand around her and drew her close. The music was Latin, with a heavy beat like a pulse, but slow and sweet. The day had been long and emotion-laden, and she sighed contentedly as she rested her head on his shoulder.

Over the past two weeks Alex had seen Marcos in many moods, but tonight's was different again. He was at his charming, sophisticated best, and the evening had taken on an enchantment. She had had little experience in dancing, but in the tight circle of his arms that didn't seem to matter. He led her effortlessly, and she followed his steps with a natural ease and lightness, as though they had been dancing together for years.

"You're enjoying yourself?" he murmured softly in her ear as the music ended.

"Yes, very much. And you?" She leaned back to look up at him—and wished she hadn't. His face was a little flushed, the expression in his eyes bold and reckless.

"I'm enjoying myself more than I can ever tell you!" He pulled her closer, and she lay against his chest until the music began again. He had removed his jacket, and now the fine silk of his shirt was against her cheek. Together they moved in perfect unison, almost like one person, and she could feel the hard male strength of him touching all along the length of her slender body. As one hand moved up and down her back with sensual langour she trembled in his hold, never wanting the music to end.

Even before the last notes died away, he drew her off the crowded floor and into the shadow of the overhanging balcony where the light of the lantern did not reach. She knew what was going to happen, and her nerves tingled in anticipation. The one kiss he had taken before had given her a glimpse of the heaven to be found in his arms, and in the secret recesses of her heart she had longed to have the kiss repeated.

He caught her close with a controlled violence that effectively annihilated her inhibitions. She didn't need the pressure of his hand under her chin prompting her to lift her face. Their lips met. A moment of tentative response—then instant, searing passion. Gone forever were her childish fantasies of love. In their place were the wild, tumultuous longings of a woman.

As he felt her abandoned response he pulled her closer until she could feel every hard, taut muscle of him. Her body seemed submerged in his, his passion an extension of her own. She wanted the kiss to go on and on and on—and her ardent young body told him so with lips parted and eager, hard breasts pressed tightly against his chest. In those magic moments she threw over a lifetime of suppression and restraint.

"Nooo," she murmured in vague protest when he finally loosened his hold and would have drawn away. She had lost all awareness of their surroundings, forgotten everything but her need for this man. Love had been a long time coming to her, and her first confused impression was that it had arrived full-blown in all its devastating intensity. But then again, perhaps the seeds had been sown many years ago when as a serious adult-child she had been caught up in the magnetic field of his personality.

He gave her one final, lingering kiss and then pushed her firmly away. "We are in a public place, *chiquita*." He laughed huskily. "This must wait until later, when we are home."

Her eyes were shining with her newly awakened love as she followed him back to the table. Her senses were heightened to the point that everything took on a new, wonderful glow. The flowers were beautiful, the music was beautiful, the old tiled tables were beautiful—and most of all Marcos was beautiful! His face held a warmth that had been long absent. His smile was full and open. His hair was mussed from her eager hands, giving him a rakish air. Oh, how she loved him!

When they reached their table, he moved

his chair beside hers so that their shoulders touched. Lázily he raised his hand and ran one finger down the side of her flushed face.

"Where has the child gone, *querida?*" he teased. "Tonight you are all woman. You fooled me well, that night when you told me it was your first kiss."

It took her a moment for the words to penetrate her giddy brain. "Hmmm?" She frowned vaguely.

"And then that day by the waterfall, I wanted to make love to you, but once again you put me off with that naïve, little-girl shyness, and you made me angry, ashamed of myself for the very adult desires I had for you. Why did you do it, Alex? Did you mean to whet my appetite even more? Did you mean to drive me wild with desire before you gave yourself to me?"

Alex felt as though she had fallen out of a plane without a parachute and was plummeting toward the ground, fully aware that the impending crash was about to destroy her illusions forever.

"I—I don't know what you mean, Marcos."

"I simply mean, my designing one, that for a month now your words have been telling me one thing, but tonight your body tells me another. You gave yourself away, my pet. No woman of the inexperience you profess could give herself to a man in a kiss as you did." His words, his tone, were soft and caressing, his whole manner teasing and indulgent, but they struck her heart like bullets. "But I don't mind the little feminine deceit," he added quickly as he saw the stricken look on her face. "After all, we were still strangers to each other. But after tonight, we will be strangers no more! When we return home, you can show me how sorry you are that we have wasted so much time!"

Sometime—Alex wasn't even sure when—Marcos had switched from English to his native Spanish, and the foreign words sounded even more lilting and seductive. His eyes held hers with an intensity that made her quiver with emotion. Surely he didn't seriously mean what he was saying!

"I—I wasn't trying to deceive you, Marcos. I—I wasn't just . . . teasing you. You *are* the first, the only man who has ever kissed me!"

"Alex, Alex, why do you insist on pretending?" he protested impatiently. "Do you think it matters to me if I am the first or the hundredth?"

The evening was warm and sultry, but Alex felt a chill of apprehension take possession of her. "What exactly are you trying to say to me, Marcos?" she asked quietly.

"I am saying that there is no need to pretend innocence with me. I am not rough with my women, no matter what their experience. I will be a gentle lover, never fear."

Before, when Marcos was trying to frighten her away, she had known that it was just a game he played, but now she could not doubt the absolute sincerity in his confident words. Sincerity—but not love, not even affection.

Even in the colored light of the lanterns Marcos saw her face pale, her soft mouth tighten with tension. "What is it, Alex?" he asked sharply. "Why do you frown? Is it my hand? Does the sight of it . . . disgust you?"

"No! No, of course not!" She was genuinely shocked by the suggestion.

"That is good! Because for the past six months I have been living the life of only half a man! That is over," he muttered fiercely. "I now have as much use of my hand as I will ever have, and I must begin to live again!"

"But not with me!" Her cry was that of a stricken child, but Marcos was beyond recognizing it as such.

"Why not with you? What could be simpler? You live in my house, we are together constantly. You are young and beautiful and very desirable—and the way you respond to a man is enough to drive him crazy!"

"But I didn't know . . . I didn't understand—"

Some of her fear communicated itself to him, and he laid a reassuring hand over her trembling ones.

"Ah, I know I have been a brute to you at times"—and he smiled the sardonic smile she hated—"and I may continue to be so when we are working. But in love, I will be very, very kind."

"What if I don't want you for a lover?" she cried desperately.

His laugh was low and disbelieving. "You are speaking to the man who held you in his arms tonight, *querida*, and felt the passion in you. You think I do not know when a woman wants me, is practically begging me to make love to her? Our surroundings were inhibiting"—he laughed with a quick glance around—"but once alone, I will again be very persuasive. Do you doubt that?"

No, she didn't! And his words conjured up such a picture that Alex quivered inside. Were she another kind of girl, the woman he supposed her, she would have flung herself into his arms once again. But she wasn't! She had been mistaken when she told Pieter that she had never dreamed, because somewhere in her heart, she realized, was her dream of love—warm, happy, passionate love, returned and fulfilled. And it bore no resemblance to this appeasement of the sensual appetites that Marcos offered her, the dubious honor of becoming his mistress because she was convenient!

"We will find much pleasure together, *mi amor*," he continued confidently.

"No!" She loved him with all her heart, but that love didn't blind her or make her fool enough to believe her love for him made his proposition possible. "Marcos, please, no more! You—you once said that I was a romantic, and—and I'm afraid I am. I'm flattered by your suggestion—"

"Flattered! *Dios!*"

"Please, Marcos! People are beginning to stare," she whispered, suddenly very much aware of the interested onlookers nearby.

"Let them stare!" But he lowered his voice. "I am not flattering you, Alex. I want you!" He reached into his pocket and threw a handful of bills on the table. "Come. We will discuss this outside."

"There's nothing to discuss!" But she allowed herself to be guided through the tables, through the flowered archway. Across the narrow, cobbled street was the entrance to a park, and he took her by the arm and led her to a deserted corner.

"So you are a romantic, are you?" he mocked. Before she could guess his intention, she was in his arms again, and though he held her so she could not escape him, he didn't hurt her as he cupped her face with one hand and turned it up to his. "What could be more romantic than this, *querida*—a tropical moon, the soft, sweet smell of flowers in the air?"

Slowly he laid his lips against the side of her neck and then in the hollow of her shoulder. His thumb moved rhythmically against her soft cheek as he plundered her exposed skin with his lips. She couldn't suppress the moan that escaped her lips as he caught the lobe of her ear between his teeth and bit gently. By the time his mouth took hers she was soft and clinging in his arms. But even as her lips surrendered to the inevitability of his kiss, one part of her mind retained its sanity.

He didn't care about her! Any woman would have done after six long months of self-imposed celibacy. She had lived all her life with no one caring about her as a person. To her father all that mattered was her talent, and now to Marcos his only concern was that she was available and presumably willing.

As Marcos felt her surrender, his hold had loosened slightly, and now Alex took advantage of that to push her hands against his chest and break away from him.

"Alex!" He sighed, reaching for her again.

"No, Marcos! You must listen to me! I won't! I won't let myself be used like this! Just because my looks are passable and it happens to suit your convenience, I—I won't let you make love to me!"

"What is it you want, *chiquita*?" He groaned in frustration.

"I don't want anything from you!"

"Ah, you are offended, perhaps"—he smiled knowingly—"because I have not praised your beauty, your charm?"

"No! No!"

Her denial sobered him, and as he looked at her mutinous face his lips twisted with contempt. "Then it is the declaration of love that you want. You want the words. Women always want the words, even when they know they are untrue. It would pacify your romantic little heart, undoubtedly, if I told you I loved you, could not live without you. Then you would come to me!"

"No, Marcos," she said with great dignity. "No, I wouldn't, because I would recognize it for the lie it was! You care nothing about me! If I were to leave tomorrow, you'd feel nothing but anger and frustration that you would have to find another pianist—preferably male next time!"

He looked slowly, deliberately, at her flushed face, tousled hair, and heaving breasts, and shrugged carelessly—that in itself an insult. "And what if it is so? Without your undeniable talent, what makes you different from any other woman? After this evening, you could convince me of nothing! You lead me on. You are all warm and melting in my arms. You virtually ask me to take you. If it is not my lovemaking, what is it you want?"

Alex had never been so hurt and humiliated in her entire life. Everything he said was true. She had discovered her love for him, and believing her feelings were returned, she had thrown herself at him. She had wanted him to kiss her, love her—desperately! How was she to know that the passion that motivated him stemmed from desire alone and not love?

She pressed her hand against her lips to stop their trembling, and Marcos saw the gesture—the mortification and chagrin on her face—and misinterpreted the reason for it. His eyes narrowed into angry slits and his lips curled with ugly contempt.

"Yes," he drawled nastily, "you wanted me for your lover! So what is stopping you now? Hmmm? Ah, I see! We have not yet come to terms, is that it? Tell me, what price do you set on your lovely body, your assumed innocence, your unfailing good nature and cooperation? Is it a diamond necklace, the promise of an apartment of your own, a car, or just the cold, hard cash? . . . Well?" he demanded as she shook her head in helpless silence. "What is it? Or don't you know yet what I am worth?"

Alex felt as though her heart and pride had been shattered into a thousand tiny splinters that pierced her very soul. "Oh, you're wrong, so wrong!" she cried.

"Little fool! Do you think I have reached the age of thirty-five without knowing every turn and trick of the female mind? I should congratulate you, for you had me fooled! This last month you have played the part of simple maid well—no coquettish batting of the eyelashes, no meaningful brushing of your hand against mine. Just your big brown eyes looking soulfully into mine. You nearly broke down, though, didn't you, the day of our outing? When you fell against me, I could feel your heart beating, your pulses racing. Oh, but you made a quick recovery. You saved it all for tonight! Did you want to make sure my hand wouldn't be totally crippled before you made your play?"

"Oh, Marcos! Marcos!" How could he speak to her like that? His heart and soul were as maimed as his two poor fingers! And she wept for him.

"Well, I have always been willing to pay for my pleasures when necessary," he continued as though she had not spoken. "So, what is it you want, my sweet?"

"Nothing!" she cried. "I want nothing from you! Now or ever!" She laughed, because her pride would not allow her to cry in front of this cynical man, but there was no humor in the sound. She laughed at her own stupid innocence; she laughed at the ignorant, idealistic girl she had once been. Later, later she would cry.

"Well, Marcos, you've at last achieved your goal. From the beginning you wanted to get rid of me, and you've finally succeeded. I'm leaving in the morning!"

He reached out, grabbing her by the upper arm, and his fingers bruised her soft flesh. "Oh, no, you are not!" he spat through clenched teeth. "You are not leaving now! I gave you every opportunity to go in the beginning, and you refused to take it! You stayed and proved yourself useful to me. Well, I won't let you leave, not now that the work is nearly completed!"

"The work! What has your work to do with this?"

"Everything! Our professional relationship has nothing to do with our . . . personal differences! You still have another month left on your contract with van Loos."

"I don't care about the contract! I'm going! And—and you can't stop me!"

"Oh, no? Your music is your profession. Leave now and I'll see that you never work again!"

His threat did not frighten her, but the wild look in his eyes did, and prudently she kept silent. Somehow in the morning she would find a way to leave San Blas, even if she had to walk all the way to Guadalajara!

Roughly he turned her and pushed her toward the car. "It is decided, then! We will hear no more talk of your leaving!"

She opened her mouth to protest but closed it again quickly as he gave her a shake.

"That is good. You will keep still," he snapped. "As you said earlier, we have nothing more to discuss!"

Chapter Six

$\mathcal{T}$he light from the window fell on the tumbled bed. Alex moaned softly in her sleep and turned onto her other side, taking the sheet with her while the rest of the covers dropped to the floor. Outside on the rail of the balcony a sea gull perched, crying in the morning breeze, but she slept on. Not even the gentle knock on the door roused her from her exhausted slumber.

The drive home from Tepic the night before had been made in stony silence with Marcos at the wheel. The house had been dark when they arrived well after midnight, and she had hurried to her room without even waiting for him to switch on the lights. The first hours she had spent pacing the room, reliving the experiences of the day.

When she had finally fallen exhausted into bed, she still could not sleep. The memories were too fresh and painful in her mind. First the tension over lunch followed by the relief in the doctor's surgery of finding that the operation had restored partial use of the hand. Then dinner, the music, the dancing, Marcos's devastating lovemaking—sheer heaven, the realization that she loved him. Finally the disillusionment of discovering how he really felt about her.

What made the aftermath worse was that, as hurt and angry as she was, she couldn't entirely blame Marcos for the disastrous end to the momentous evening. So much of it was her fault, she acknowledged with a groan. If she hadn't invited his kisses and then responded with such abandon to his practiced lovemaking—stupid, naïve, blundering fool that she was! No wonder he had doubted her innocence! She must have seemed— obviously did seem—like a ripe plum just waiting to be plucked. No, she had corrected herself a little hysterically, not a plum in Mexico. A ripe mango just waiting to be plucked! Even with her lack of practical experience, she had read enough to know that a man's passion was easily aroused, and that such passion had little to do with the warm, giving, flowering love that had motivated her response.

Here was a man who hadn't been with a woman for months and months, and with the first kiss she had behaved like a—a wanton! She had made a fool of herself, albeit innocently. Oh, how could she ever face him again! But she didn't want to leave! Desperately she wanted to stay. She couldn't bear the thought of giving up their work, of parting from him. . . .

As her thoughts had grown more confused and incoherent, her tired body finally prevailed over her seething brain, and just as dawn broke she had fallen into a heavy—thankfully dreamless—sleep.

The knock sounded on the door once more, this time louder, and still Alex did not awaken, but she stirred just a little and one foot found its way out from under the sheet into the cool morning air. She was oblivious to the dark form that slipped through the door into her room and stood hesitating, watching her as she slept.

"Alex!" Marcos's whisper was low and urgent—and she slept on.

"Alex!" Quietly he crossed the room and bent over her sleeping form. "Alex!" he repeated. Nothing.

Gently, so as not to startle her, he sat on the side of the large bed and laid a hand on her shoulder. "Alex!" More urgently now.

"Not yet, Ruthy," she mumbled, turning away from the hand. "Lemme sleep just a little longer."

As she shifted position the sheet fell away, revealing a smooth expanse of leg from ankle to thigh. Her sheer nylon gown had ridden up to her hips and one strap had fallen off her tanned shoulder. Her hair was a riot of curls around her pale face, leaving most of it concealed. Marcos gave one rueful glance at her dishabille and carefully covered up the exposed leg before reaching out and touching her bare shoulder more firmly.

"Alex! Wake up! I need to talk to you!" Gently he shook her until her eyes slowly opened, sleepy and dazed. She blinked and tried to focus on the blurred face swimming above her. She must still be asleep, she thought vaguely. It looked for all the world like Marcos.

Marcos! In an instant she was wide awake, her mouth open ready to scream, but before the sound was born, his hand clamped tightly over her lips.

"Shhh! Please, Alex! I must speak with you!"

Frantically she grabbed at the sheet and pulled it up over her breasts, covered now by nothing but a frothy bit of blue nylon.

"I'm sorry I startled you, but I had to talk to you before you came downstairs," he explained. "I'll take my hand away, but please, be quiet!"

Alex's eyes above his fingers stared at him, wide and bewildered, as he slowly lifted the pressure. A good share of her most painful thoughts the previous night had been given to imagining their first encounter today, and not even her wildest fantasies had conjured up anything like this! She had pictured him as cold and distant, furious with her still. She had imagined the meeting filled with embarrassment, hostility, constraint. And now here he sat on the edge of her bed in a silk dressing gown, his face haggard, his unshaven jaw grim and set, his eyes dark and brooding.

"What—what is it, Marcos?" she stammered.

"We have company! They came yesterday while we were away. Tomás was waiting up to tell me when we got home."

"Who is it?" Whoever it was had obviously upset him badly, and he looked as though he had not slept at all.

"My aunt," he said tersely, "and my cousin Elena, her daughter-in-law."

"You didn't know they were coming?"

"No!" As he rose and began to pace around the room Alex pulled herself to a sitting position, the sheet tucked under her chin. "Sophie has telephoned often," he continued, "wanting to come, and I thought that I had successfully discouraged her. And I have an excellent idea who put her up to it now!"

She watched the angry muscle work in the side of his throat as he clenched and unclenched his good fist. "What's the problem?" she asked cautiously. "Do they expect you to entertain them?"

"No, no!" he muttered distractedly. "You don't understand."

Alex leaned weakly back against the pillows. This whole situation had the unreal quality of a dream. "Is there something you want me to understand?" she asked carefully, feeling that at the least wrong word he would explode.

"Yes! No! . . . I don't know!" he mumbled and dropped back beside her on the bed.

"Do—do they know I'm here?"

"No, Tomás was very discreet."

Discreet! Suddenly Alex thought she saw the problem. "Ohhh, I see. I've become a bit of an embarrassment, is that it? Do you want me to hide in my room until they're gone?" she offered dryly.

"No, of course not!" he snapped. "Do you think I care what they think? Besides, my aunt would certainly understand . . ." His voice trailed off lamely.

". . . if you had a woman living with you?" Alex finished for him tartly. If Marcos had had his way last night, whatever his aunt's conjectures might be, they would have probably been the truth! The thought of meeting his relatives in such circumstances made her shudder, and she realized that it was going to be awkward enough as it was. "So what do you want me to do?"

"Just leave the talking to me. They know nothing about my work, and that's the way I want to keep it."

"How do you plan to explain my presence?"

"I don't know. I'll think of something."

"So wouldn't it be better if I just left? They would never have to know I was ever here," she offered gruffly.

"No! You cannot leave me. Especially not

now! I need you more than ever! I realize the situation isn't pleasant," he conceded, "but, Alex, I meant what I said last night. You are not to go!" His voice was suddenly more gentle as he smoothed the hair from her forehead. "Why don't you stay up here for a while and let me greet them first. I'll have Tomás bring you some breakfast."

He stood and turned to leave, but not toward the hall. Instead, he went to a door next to the wardrobe that had always been kept locked; Alex had assumed that it was a closet or storage room. Now she realized that it connected to Marcos's room next door! As though he read her mind, he paused as he opened it and transferred the large iron key from his side to hers. "There! You can lock it after me. I wouldn't want you to worry," he said grimly.

After he had gone, Alex stared thoughtfully after him. Intuition told her that there was more to this than Marcos was revealing. The visitors had disturbed something more fundamental in him than his desire for solitude. She had had no experience with relatives, and she knew that often there was no love lost within families, but his reaction to their arrival seemed out of proportion to the event. There was definitely some mystery behind all this, and he was right. She couldn't leave him now, desert him in what she suspected were troubled times ahead for him. It was not going to be easy, loving him as she did. But he would never know, and right now his need was greater than her pride.

A sharp knock on the door announced Tomás's arrival with her meal, and one look at his face told her that he was also troubled by the new arrivals.

"I understand we have company," she said casually as he set the tray on the bedside table.

"Yes, Señora Ortega came yesterday afternoon," he said somberly. "She is a very nice lady. Her husband died many years ago, and Señor Marcos is very fond of her."

He turned to go, but Alex stopped him. "And the other lady, her daughter-in-law?"

Tomás paused, his back still to her. "That one! She is— Never mind! You will see for yourself. But watch out for that one, *niña*. Señora Elena is not going to like finding you here!"

With that warning he left Alex to her own thoughts. Elena Ortega, she mused as she sipped her chocolate. Surely she had heard that name before. She had a vivid memory of the picture of Marcos with a strikingly beautiful Mexican woman. The gossip columns had linked their names together a year or so ago. She also remembered Marcos's reaction when she had alluded to the woman. Could she be part of his past that had made him so bitter?

On impulse Alex took greater pains with her appearance than usual. Ordinarily she would have just donned jeans and a shirt over her swimsuit so she could spend the morning on the beach. Today, instead, she chose white slacks and an embroidered silk blouse in her favorite shades of blues and greens. She brushed her hair until it shone with copper lights and applied a light makeup. Like a warrior on the way to battle, she thought with a smile.

At the bottom of the stairs, she hesitated, and the sound of voices drew her to the sitting room. A deep, husky voice was saying in lilting Spanish, "So if you wouldn't come to us, *Madre* and I decided to come to you."

In the doorway Alex stopped and looked at the scene. The woman who had spoken was sitting with her back to the door in a high chair that hid her from view. To her right on the sofa was an older, comfortably plump woman dressed entirely in black, presumably Marcos's aunt. Marcos himself stood by the fireplace, his arm resting on the mantel. As she entered, his eyes held hers with such a look of frustrated anger that she felt all the protective instincts rise in her.

"Let me warn you," Elena continued, "that we will do everything possible to pry you away from this . . . this shocking ruin and take you back to the *hacienda* with us."

"You must see, Marcos," Señora Ortega added softly, "that this way of life just won't do at all, living here all by yourself when you know that nothing would please me more than coddling you a little."

Marcos winced almost perceptibly and forced a smile to his lips. "Ah, but, Sophie, you're mistaken. I'm not alone. I have the best companion in the world." And then to Alex: "Come in, my dear. You must meet my aunt whom I have told you so much about. Oh, and my cousin Elena, of course."

As he held out his hand to her both women turned in their seats with different degrees of surprise registering in their faces. His aunt's held interest and some bewilderment, but Elena Ortega gave every indication of fury. Warily Alex crossed the room to take his hand. His eyes held a warning, but that did not prepare her adequately for his next words.

"Sophie, Elena, I would like you to meet Alex—my wife."

It was fortunate that he had slipped his arm around her waist just before making his preposterous announcement, or Alex was sure she would have fallen.

"Your wife!" the two women exclaimed in unison, covering her own gasp of dismay.

"My dear, that is wonderful news," Sophie Ortega exclaimed with genuine pleasure. "When? Where? Oh, Marcos, why didn't you tell me!"

"We've been married just a week, and I waited to call you until after the splints were removed. If the news had been bad, I wanted

143

to temper it with some good news," he lied glibly.

By now Alex had had a little time to recover from the shock, and she didn't need Marcos's fingers biting into her side to keep her quiet. Had she been given the opportunity in the first moment, she would have blurted out a denial, but now, if nothing else, the expression on Elena Ortega's face held her silent. The woman was not just stunned or unhappy, she was furiously angry, and the look she gave Alex was filled with such venom that Alex drew back into Marcos's encircling arm.

"Oh, Marcos," Sophie continued. "I am so happy for you! My son Ramón, Elena's husband," she explained to Alex, "and Marcos were best of friends all their lives. Marcos has been so good to us since he died. . . ." She paused and raised a black-edged handkerchief to her lips.

"Please, Sophie, don't upset yourself," he said gently.

"It is just that even after two years, it is so hard for me to forget. . . . Ah, Marcos, I don't know what I would do without you! That is why it was so hard for me to understand when you would not come to the *hacienda* when you were injured. It would have given me a chance to do something for you."

"Now, we've been through all that, Sophie," he chided. "It is better for me to be here, away from everyone." He smiled down

144

at Alex. "Alex will tell you that I haven't been easy to live with. Isn't that so, my dear?"

Alex opened her lips to speak and closed them again. What could she say that wouldn't get her hopelessly embroiled in this tangle? If she wasn't already!

"Tell us . . . Alex, is it?" Elena drawled. "How did you and Marcos happen to meet in this . . . this hole?"

"Now, Elena, dear," her mother-in-law interrupted anxiously, "I am sure Marcos will tell us everything in his own good time."

"Oh, come, *Madre*"—she smiled sweetly—"surely that isn't too personal a question, and I'm fascinated to learn what means she used to trap our elusive hermit." She turned a bright, malicious smile on Alex. "Did you come here as a maid, dear?"

Alex stared uncomprehending for a moment and then realized that she had tanned so darkly over the past month that Elena took her for a native of these parts and meant to be deliberately insulting. But Alex was more amused than offended by the woman's patronizing rudeness, and her sense of humor got the better of her.

"*Sí, señora*," Alex replied in husky Spanish. "I came as a maid and stayed to clean up. You should try it some time."

"Alex!" Marcos exclaimed, but his lips twitched at Elena's stunned expression.

"I'm sorry, Marcos." Alex laughed. "I just

couldn't resist. Actually, Señora Ortega," she continued in Spanish as cultured as Elena's own, "Marcos and I met years ago in London, but our careers took us different ways. We renewed our acquaintance recently through Marcos's manager, Pieter van Loos."

"Oh!" Sophie exclaimed, beaming with satisfaction as Elena glowered. "Are you a musician, too? How lovely!"

"But then, Marcos is no longer a musician, is he?" Elena snapped nastily. "His career is finished. Does she know that you have a cattle ranch that is waiting for you to return and assume your responsibilities?"

Marcos had gone pale at Elena's first cruel words, but he rallied quickly. "You are beating an old horse to death, Elena. Carlos manages just fine without me."

"What is this dead horse?" Sophie asked, puzzled. "I assure you, Marcos, that the animals are all very healthy."

A fond smile curved his lips. "I'm sure they are, Sophie. Carlos does an excellent job. That is why I'm not inclined to interfere. I would make a mess of running the ranch."

"Just what do you plan to do?" Elena interrupted. "Surely you don't intend to stay here! Why, you're totally cut off from civilization!"

"Which is why I was so surprised that you would choose this for your vacation spot, dear cousin," he said dryly. "Alex and I have no trouble at all finding things to do to amuse ourselves—day and night." The implication in his tone was too clear to be misunderstood, and both Alex and Elena flushed a bright red.

"I should think not!" His aunt chuckled softly. "Alex is a very lovely woman. Come here, my dear, and tell me about yourself. I detect an accent, though you speak our language very well. Are you American?"

Hesitantly Alex freed herself from Marcos's grasp. What was she doing? By not denying his announcement immediately, she had tacitly agreed to his deception. How long did he mean for it to go on? Well, to save his pride, she wouldn't denounce him now, but she was not going to allow it to go on for long! He would have to explain that it was all a little joke!

Marcos must have read her thoughts, for before he released her, he murmured for her ears alone: "We'll sort this out later, Alex!"

The next hour was one of the worst of Alex's life. Between Señora Ortega's gentle questions and Elena's barbed comments, she was nearly at her wits' end when Marcos called a halt.

"I'm afraid I must take Alex away now. We have some business to attend to before lunch. Just make yourselves at home, and ask Tomás for anything you need." He held out his hand to her, and for once she was grateful to be led by the autocratic man. In the music room, he closed and locked the door.

"Now!" he said purposefully. "You may as well sit down and make yourself comfortable."

"You're going to have to tell them the truth, Marcos," she stated wearily as she collapsed onto the sofa. "I didn't want to call you a liar to your face, but I won't let this go on any longer. I've never felt like such a cheat in my life!"

"It's too late, Alex," he said quietly.

"Too late! But it's a lie! What made you do it?"

"Because it was the only way I could think of to be rid of that daughter of Lucifer once and for all!"

His voice was filled with loathing, and Alex wasn't naïve enough to think he meant his aunt. This was not just dislike. His feelings about Elena went much deeper than that. On his face she saw that same deep hatred she had seen once before and hoped never to see again.

"So she is the woman," she murmured. She had spoken to herself, but Marcos heard.

"What do you know?" he snapped. "What did Pieter tell you?"

"Why—why, nothing," she stuttered. "I—I only guessed. She's the woman whose picture I saw with yours in the paper, obviously the one who's made you so . . . well, bitter."

"Bitter!" His laugh was ugly. "Bitter is a mild word to express what I feel when I look at her! First she ruined my cousin's life, and then she ruined mine!"

"I—I don't understand."

Alex watched him with wide, nervous eyes as he began to prowl the room. The veneer of civilization seemed to have been stripped from him, leaving a man as dangerous and as unpredictable as a snarling jungle cat as he said:

"You will understand when I tell you about my so precious cousin. And she is my cousin, several times removed. She was orphaned at fifteen and my father brought her to live on the *hacienda,* for her branch of the family was poor. There were four of us all near the same age—myself, my younger brother Carlos, Ramón, and Elena. For a while we were all infatuated with her, and as she grew older she took great delight in playing us off, one against the other. I was the eldest, and as I pursued my career, gained more experience with women, I came to see her for the greedy, grasping female she was—just like all others."

"Not all women are like that!" Alex felt stung into replying.

"No? You must forgive me if I can't agree with you."

His temper was so uncertain that Alex didn't dare argue the point, at least not then. "So what about Elena?" she prompted.

"Elena wanted the security of marriage,

and she would have had me if she could. Oh, don't think me conceited; it is just that I was my father's heir. But as time went on and I remained elusive, she chose Ramón."

"Did—did she love him?"

"Love! What she loved was the rather substantial inheritance his father had left him. But he was a gentle man—which she considered weakness—and soon she became bored with poor Ramón. And I had to stand back and watch while she made his life a hell! No one will ever convince me that the car crash that killed him was an accident. He knew that mountain road too well."

"You—you believe that Elena drove her husband to suicide? That's why you're so bitter?"

"That in itself would be enough, but no! With Ramón dead, she began her pursuit of me. To become mistress of *Rancho Rivera* became an obsession with her once my father died. A year ago she began following me on my concert tours. For my aunt's sake, I was civil to her. That was a mistake. She mistook civility for encouragement. She considered my career the only obstacle to achieving her goal. She was convinced that, without my music, I would return to assume control of the *hacienda* and marry her. As the weeks passed she became insanely jealous of my playing."

"Is—is she a little mad?" Alex asked hesitantly.

"Mad? No! Selfish, ambitious, greedy. She has lived on her wits all her life and has learned to manipulate people so well that she now believes she can have anything she wants."

"Including you."

"Including me!"

For a long moment he sat staring at his crippled hand. Her eyes followed his to the two useless fingers, and a chill ran down her spine.

"What happened to your hand, Marcos?" she asked with a nameless premonition of something horrible to come.

"No one but Pieter knows the truth," he said coldly, his eyes hard. "And if ever you reveal what I am about to tell you, you will curse the day you were born."

"You have my word, Marcos," she promised solemnly.

He continued to stare in her direction, but she knew that he was seeing an inner vision. "Last October," he began slowly, "I was playing two weeks in Paris. Elena had followed me. I had just heard from Pieter that he had arranged a three months' residency for me in Vienna, performing and teaching master classes. Elena was furious because it meant that I had no intention of giving up my career.

"We were at a party given by some mutual friends, and she maneuvered me into driving her home. All the way back to the hotel we quarreled about my music, about Ramón, until finally I lost my temper. Despite my regard for Sophie, in no uncertain terms I told her how I felt about her—my loathing for her. You will think I should have done it before, but she was still my cousin, and with my father dead, as head of the family I was responsibile for her, even though I believed she had forfeited the right to any consideration."

Yes, Alex thought with a wave of love and pride, whatever else Marcos might be, he was not a man to shirk what he felt was a responsibility. He had too much honor, too much pride of family. She saw the pain deep in his eyes and prompted gently, "What happened?"

"When we arrived in front of her hotel, she asked me if I would at least have the decency to walk her through the lobby. She got out before I could help her and came around the car. I had opened the door on my side—"

He paused, and when he continued, his voice was devoid of all emotion, but beads of perspiration had gathered on his forehead. "As I took the keys out of the ignition, I accidentally dropped them, and they fell on the floor on the far side of the car. I took hold of the top of the doorframe to brace myself and reached down for them.

"In that instant, Elena slammed the car door on my hand!"

Chapter Seven

Alex sat in stunned silence, hardly able to breathe. The accident to Marcos's hand had been no accident at all! She thought of that poor hand as she had seen it yesterday when it first came out of the splints—so pale and useless, the faint lines of the scars across the back, the two fingers forever lifeless. She thought of the years of playing he had had ahead of him, the pleasure he had brought to so many millions of people. All that gone because of a vicious, vindictive woman. That another human being could do such a thing was sick—criminal!

She closed her eyes and fought a rising nausea. It was almost too much for her mind to fathom. But why had Marcos allowed Elena to get away with it, to escape some kind of retribution? She felt his weight sink onto the sofa beside her, and she turned her head to see his face, white and lined but under tight control.

"So perhaps now you can understand a little of how I feel," he said curtly.

153

"And—and you told no one but Pieter how it happened?"

"I had to keep it out of the papers at all costs. My first thought was to avoid a scandal —for my aunt, for my family's sake. The damage had already been done to my hand, my career. No vengeance on my part could have brought back those lifeless nerves. Oh, it would have given me the greatest pleasure and satisfaction to have publicly denounced Elena for what she is—but the cost to Sophie would have been too great, and I could not have lived with that on my conscience."

"But why? Your aunt loves you deeply!"

"Which is all the more reason for her never to find out that it was not an accident!" He read the disbelief in her troubled eyes and said impatiently, "Alex, Sophie has suffered so much in her life. She has lost nearly everyone closest and dearest to her. Her husband died as a young man from a congenital heart ailment. Six years ago my father, her only brother, died. And then the strange circumstances of Ramón's death nearly killed her. He was her only child, her whole reason for being. But she is a kind, simple woman, and she never saw what Elena was doing to him. Now all her affection has been transferred to her daughter-in-law. For me to destroy her faith in Elena would be criminal in itself!"

Alex felt her heart wrench in pain. Marcos might be bitter and cynical about women, but heaven knew he had just cause! "So what do you mean to do now?" she asked to break the silence.

"With your help, I will be rid of Elena's pursuit once and for all!" he said sharply. "Once she knows that I am . . . unattainable, she must turn elsewhere. As long as I remained unmarried, she always had the hope that I would turn to her."

"Even after what she did to you?" she asked incredulously.

He shrugged. "That is the price I paid for remaining silent about her part in my 'accident.' She can delude herself that I did it out of feeling for her! But after this morning, I hope to heaven that she finally sees that any hopes are useless."

Alex's face was pale as she watched the play of emotions across his face. "Did you plan your—your announcement about our supposed marriage beforehand?" she asked quietly.

"No. I didn't think of it until I looked up and saw you standing in the doorway. Elena greeted me this morning as though nothing were wrong between us, as though the incident in Paris had never occurred. It made me sick!" he spat. "But my aunt was there and I couldn't say anything. It was all I could do to restrain myself from throwing her bodily out of my house! The woman has no conscience, no guilt, no shame."

Alex had learned all she needed to know— all she wanted to know. His revelations about

Elena had appalled her, and she was at a loss to know what to do next about her own entanglement in the affair.

"So—so you want me to pretend to be your wife for the duration of their stay, is that it?" she asked hesitantly. "But then what? You can't continue the charade indefinitely."

He looked at her through narrowed eyes, his face hard and set. "No," he said slowly. "No, I can't pretend indefinitely, nor do I intend to."

"Oh, you think she'll marry again soon herself." She nodded.

A grim smile played around the corners of his mouth. "That wasn't quite what I meant," he drawled. "I meant that I do not intend for our marriage to be a pretense!"

Once again Alex was stunned into silence, though after all that had occurred this morning, she thought wildly, she didn't know why anything he said or did should surprise her!

"I—I think you'd better explain," she said carefully.

He shrugged. "It is quite simple. We will marry."

"Marry!" She raised a hand to her heart as though to stop its erratic pounding.

"Of course! In Mexico marriage is easily arranged. Sometime in the next day or so, we will go into San Blas to the padre there. We can be married and return home without anyone's knowing."

He made it sound like the most natural thing in the world!

"I'm afraid that I would know!" she sputtered.

"Naturally!" And his lips twitched in sardonic amusement.

How dare he find anything amusing in this preposterous situation! she thought indignantly. Once Marcos had explained the circumstances to her, she could understand the reasons behind his absurd announcement. And, heaven help her, she had even found herself considering the possibility of continuing the deception. But marriage in such circumstances! Oh, that was quite something else, indeed! And he outlined his plans with all the assurance in the world that she would fall in with them!

"Well, I won't do it! I—I might consider pretending to be . . . to be—"

"My wife?" he supplied helpfully when the words stuck in her throat.

"Yes!" she gasped. "I might, just might, consider that—for a little while anyway. But to carry it so far as a phony marriage—"

"Oh, there would be nothing phony—as you so delicately put it—about it! We would be married by the laws of the state and the church," he announced firmly.

"Well, I won't do it! This is preposterous!"

"Why?" he drawled lazily, his eyes roving up and down her tense figure to her irate face.

"You know why!" she snapped. "One doesn't just—just blunder into marriage because it happens to be convenient!"

"Convenient! You are very fond of that word, my dear—"

"I'm not your dear anything!" she cried, knowing she spoke the truth.

"—and I'm beginning to find it annoying," he continued, ignoring the interruption. "I would prefer to say that a marriage between us would be advantageous—to both of us."

"You're mad! You don't even like me!"

"I don't like any woman, with the possible exception of my unworldly aunt, but that has little to do with expediency."

"Well, I don't happen to be interested in making an *expedient* marriage!"

"Why not?" he asked tersely, his eyes narrowing. "Do you fancy yourself in love with someone already?"

"That's no business of yours! And that's beside the point! I'm not interested in marriage to anyone!" she said untruthfully. "I—I have my career to consider."

"Good! Now we are getting somewhere!"

His complacency shook her, and she eyed him suspiciously. "What do you mean?"

"I mean," he retorted nastily, "that I recognize that there must be something for you in this marriage. I never imagined for a moment that you'd go into it for altruistic reasons. What I suggest is a little quid pro quo— something for something."

"I thought we had this out last night!" She would have risen to her feet, but Marcos restrained her with a bruising hand on her arm.

"There's no need to display your whole range of indignation and outraged pride. I'll take it as read so that we can get down to business."

"I don't want to hear any more!" she cried furiously. "In the last two days you have insulted me in practically every conceivable way, and now you expect me to listen to you?"

"And do you expect me to apologize for last night? You don't consider that you asked for just what you got?"

"Oh, you're impossible!" But she subsided weakly back against the cushions. Her love for him was too strong and his personality too forceful for her to fight for very long. Just his touch left her weak and trembling, and she fought for breath. "Okay, say what you have to say and be done with it!"

"That is hardly encouraging," he murmured.

"Oh, go on!"

He gave her a moment to regain her composure and then continued mildly. "After the accident I had no intention of ever marrying, and I have no desire now for a wife in the accepted sense of the word. The little woman bustling around the house, soothing my furrowed brow in times of distress—that holds no allure for me. But the protection of a wife somewhere in the offing to ward away persistent females does. I'm not asking you to live with me for any length of time, just long enough to finish the suite and get rid of Elena."

"I don't want to hear any more of this!" Alex cried. His words were the most heartless, the most callous, she could ever imagine.

"But you will!" he said coldly. "I'm just coming to the part that will interest you. You say I don't like you, but for all that, you must admit you command my respect—at least professionally. We work well together; the last month has demonstrated that. And the future could hold a great deal of promise for us in collaboration. I will tell you frankly, that is more than I ever expected to say to any woman! You can be of great use to me—and I in turn can be of great use to you."

"I remember you asked my price last night!" she retorted, still stung by the memory.

"Last night you made me lose my temper. In spite of what I said, in thinking it over I don't believe you're a mercenary woman," he observed shrewdly. "Quite honestly, if that were the case, I would simply try to buy your cooperation. However, I think I can offer you something which you do value."

Alex looked at him reclining so confidently, so self-assured. If the matter didn't strike so near to her heart, she could have laughed in his face. Not for a moment did she believe he knew the only thing he could offer her which she would value—his love!

"Go on," she prompted sardonically. "I can't wait to see what you consider my price."

"I offer you something more than mere money can buy. I offer you a career."

"A career!"

"At least the potential for one," he amended. "And few men can give you that. You say you're not interested in marriage, so I would think that would suit you fine."

"I—I don't understand," she said, genuinely perplexed.

"Just this. You help me through this difficult time, help me get rid of Elena, work through to the finish of *Night Suite*, and I'll see that you get your chance to be heard by the critics. My name still carries a great deal of weight in the music world."

"What—what makes you think I care enough about a career to want it at the price of my freedom?" she asked gruffly.

"I wouldn't be depriving you of your freedom. I wouldn't ask that you live with me for more than a few months of the year when my work demands it." He smiled coldly. "You could consider yourself a part-time wife, as it were, free to go your own way as I'll go mine. What would you be sacrificing? A lifetime of playing in nightclubs"—he nearly spat the word—"churches, perhaps an occasional job as an accompanist? No, my dear, I've worked with you for over a month now. I've watched your face as you play. You are . . . what shall I say? Transformed by your music. You're never happier than when you lose yourself at the piano. You see, I would be doing you a favor! Pieter doesn't seem inclined to help you. You have no name, no family, no money, no other connections. Well, I can give those to you!"

Alex longed to contradict him, to tell him her real identity, throw his words back in his face. Oh, how Pieter would have laughed to have heard her described so! But something— she didn't even know what—held her silent. Surely she wasn't seriously considering this ridiculous proposition—part-time wife, indeed!

She didn't need any of the things he was offering her. . . . Suddenly she saw with a strange insight that, perversely, that was *why* she was considering it. She didn't need Marcos's side of the bargain, but he did need hers! She would not be selling herself, because she would never use what he offered her.

"Then—then what you're suggesting," she asked huskily, "is no marriage at all in the accepted sense? It would be in name only—for business purposes?"

"Did I really say that?" And for the first time that morning he smiled a real smile—a smile that sent her heart doing flip-flops.

"That's what you implied."

"Then the implication is at fault!"

Alex wasn't looking at him or she would have seen the gleam in his eyes. Her first warning of what was in his mind was when she felt his fingers trailing up and down her arm.

"Do you really think a strictly platonic marriage, even for brief periods of time, would satisfy either of us?" he asked softly. "You are very much a woman, and I am very much a man. We've already found out neither of us finds the other repulsive."

He was leaning toward her, supporting his weight with one arm on the back of the couch. He seemed to move forward in slow motion, and she watched in fascination as his face came nearer and nearer. He wasn't touching her when his lips finally took hers. The kiss alone joined them, but Alex felt as captive as though he held her tightly in his arms. His mouth was soft and seductive on hers, teasing, tantalizing, but not satisfying. She moaned softly in frustration and would have moved nearer, but he restrained her with a hand on her shoulder.

As slowly as he had taken the kiss he released her.

"You see?" he murmured. "A passionless union would satisfy neither of us. It would lead to nothing but frustration."

He had demonstrated his point well, and Alex was shaken by the emotions he had aroused in her and left unfulfilled. But still she couldn't contemplate what he was suggesting. Oh, he wanted her, and, to her shame and despair, she wanted him! But she knew that in his heart he had only disdain for her, for all women. She would have willingly given her soul into his keeping for a real marriage, but he could offer her nothing but a career! No, if they married . . .

Oh, what was she even thinking! How had she allowed her thoughts to take her this far? The whole notion was absurd!

"I can't!" she cried and tore herself off the sofa to put as much distance between them as possible. "I—I can't!" she whispered helplessly.

He was half reclining on the couch, watching her heaving breasts and quivering mouth with hard speculation. She couldn't stand that cold, calculating look in his eyes. As she turned away to stare out the window he levered himself off the couch and crossed silently to her. She felt his nearness even before he put his hands on her shoulders to turn her around to face him.

"What frightens you, Alex?" he said caressingly. "Am I so different from other men you've known?"

"I—I've never known any other men—not in the way you mean!" she cried. "Oh, why won't you believe me!"

He stared down into her flushed face, her eyes bright now with unshed tears, and a frown creased his brow. "Do you still persist in this pose of innocence?"

"It's no pose!" Her earnest face pleaded for his understanding. "Marcos, I've lived a very sheltered life. The world you've lived in, the kind of women you've known, the demands you would make on me are something I know nothing about. Please, can't you believe that?"

His frown deepened as he searched her face, her eyes. "I believe you're serious," he said slowly.

"Of course I'm serious! That's what I've been trying to tell you! Last night— If last night I led you to think something else, I'm sorry! You—you will have to blame it on my inexperience"—she smiled tremulously—"and your not inconsiderable experience. I wasn't trying to tease you or lead you on or bargain with you for anything. I—I just didn't know . . . I didn't realize . . ." She trailed off lamely.

Not even the cynical, jaded Marcos Rivera could doubt her sincerity. She looked too much like a frightened, bewildered child.

"All right," he said slowly, "I believe you. But where does that leave us?"

"I—I couldn't marry you letting you think I would be willing to let you make love to me."

"But you would be willing to go through with the marriage otherwise?" he asked quickly.

"I—I didn't mean that!" Alex suddenly felt like a cornered animal. Oh, how had the situation gotten so out of hand?

"What if I agreed," he persisted, "that at least temporarily you should share my home, my work—but not my bed?"

"But—but you said yourself it wouldn't work!" she gasped.

His eyes never left her face as he raised a hand and ran one finger down her soft cheek. "Poor baby, caught in the grown-up world," he mocked gently. "But you will have to grow up someday, and I'm willing to wait. You may not believe it, but I am capable of self-control when I choose."

"You—you mean you wouldn't . . . wouldn't touch me?" she asked skeptically.

His lips twitched at her obvious disbelief. "I didn't quite say that," he drawled. "I wouldn't, however . . . force myself on you. But I reserve the right to be as persuasive as possible." His hand curved around her neck, and she felt the gentle, insidious pressure of his long, artistic fingers.

"No!" she cried and turned her head frantically back and forth. Instantly the caressing touch was gone as his hands dropped lightly to her shoulders.

"You see?" he said easily. "That's all you need to say. A simple no, and I stop. What more could you expect? I'm willing to wait, you see, until you admit to yourself that you have passions and desires also."

"So what are you suggesting?" she asked weakly.

"I'm saying that if you agree to go through with this marriage, I will give you whatever time you want to become reconciled to . . . er . . . the physical aspects of being my wife."

His wife! Alex trembled and closed her eyes against the sight of his firm mouth, the sardonic gleam in his eye, the wave of hair that had fallen down over his forehead—and the darkness behind her eyes made no difference. She could still see him so clearly. And worse. Against her shoulder she could feel the three good fingers of his left hand.

What had she thought that first night when she had played for him? That she would dedicate half her life to help him if she could. And now she was being called upon to do just that. Only *half* her life, when she would willingly given him *all!* She was caught, and she could have laughed at her own folly if it weren't so tragic.

Somehow she had come to love this brooding, brilliant, enigmatic man, and whatever he wanted from her, needed from her, her heart found it impossible to deny him.

That was what had kept her silent as she listened to his ridiculous proposition. She wanted desperately to be his wife, to have the right to be near him, with him; to help him in any way she could.

Slowly she opened her eyes and looked up into his beloved face, so dark and expectant above hers. It was all she could do to hide the love in her eyes when she sensed his tension as he waited for her reply.

"All right, Marcos," she said quietly. "Under those conditions, I'll marry you."

His relief was tangible, and his hands on her shoulders tightened convulsively. "To-morrow, if I can arrange it?" he insisted. "Will you marry me tomorrow?"

"Tomorrow," she repeated softly. "I'll marry you tomorrow."

Chapter Eight

*A*lex sighed and slipped farther down into the soothing water, sending a cascade of bubbles over the edge of the bathtub. In all her years of traveling, performing, and traveling again, she had never felt so nervous and high-strung and just plain exhausted.

Dinner the night before had been an ordeal as the family party assembled for the first time. Elena had made every effort to monopolize the conversation with her witty, slightly malicious repartee, demanding and holding Marcos's attention. And just as love had come swiftly and unheralded to Alex, she had felt the first stirrings of a new and equally potent emotion—jealousy! How could she expect to compete with such a woman? For Elena was not just striking or attractive, she was devastatingly beautiful. Her complexion was flawless, her thick black hair luxurious, her figure enough to turn any man's head. Over the years she had developed the art of femininity to the nth degree. Her whole aura was one of sensuality. What hope did Alex have that Marcos would ever come to love her with such a woman around?

This morning, however, he had held her to her promise. Before the sun was up, Tomás had driven them to the old white stucco church in the village, and there Marcos had made her his wife. Over her head she wore a white lace mantilla that had belonged to his mother, and on her finger he had placed an ornate gold band set with a single diamond, also his mother's.

"She died when I was sixteen," he had told her, and she sensed the pain behind the words.

"Will—will you write Pieter and tell him what we've done?" she had asked gruffly.

For the first time that morning, a smile had curved Marcos's lips. "You make it sound as though we've robbed a bank, *chiquita*. And as a matter of fact, I called him last night."

"Was he surprised?"

"I don't know if surprised is the right word," he observed dryly.

"What did he say?"

"Oh, he had a great deal to say, some of it quite unrepeatable. Primarily it was along the lines of he would break my other hand if I did not treat you well. You have quite a champion there."

Dear Pieter! Alex thought longingly as she closed her eyes and leaned her head against the back of the bathtub. Oh, she was so tired!

She had never lived through a day like this, filled as it was with surface amiability barely concealing the tension and hostility beneath. Only Sophie seemed to be blissfully unaware of the undercurrents.

Two hours until dinner, Alex thought morosely, and if she didn't quiet her nerves, she was going to be hysterical before the end of the salad course! What did Marcos intend to do? They hadn't had a minute alone all day to make plans.

No sooner had the thought flitted through her mind than the door opened and Marcos strode purposefully into the room.

"Oh!" she screamed and made the mistake of submerging into the water with her mouth still open. "What—what are you doing in here?" she sputtered, the water in her mouth ruining the forcefulness of her indignation.

"I knocked twice," he said curtly. "I was afraid that you had drowned yourself!"

His concern was genuine, but Alex noted balefully that his interest quickly became focused on the swirling bubbles.

"I'm—I'm perfectly all right!" she stammered, surreptitiously swishing the bubbles away from the sides of the tub and toward the center.

"Yes," he drawled, studying her with a new possessiveness. "I can see you are perfectly all right. In fact, you are just perfect!" And he leaned his shoulder against the wall and let his eyes rove freely from the damp curls framing her hot face to her toes just visible above the bubbles.

"Please, Marcos, leave!" she pleaded, hardly daring to breathe for fear of disturbing her foamy covering.

"I have no intention of leaving until I talk with you," he said coldly. "I will not have Elena coiling her suffocating tentacles around me the way she did last night. You will not again withdraw into the background and let her have her own way!"

The injustice of this accusation banished her embarrassment. "Are you blaming me?" Alex gasped. "You have a mind of your own! She couldn't force you to take her for a walk in the moonlight!"

"What did you expect me to do with Sophie smiling benignly on us all!"

"And what did you expect me to do? Deny you permission to leave the room?"

"You could have come with us!"

"Oh, yes, and leave Sophie alone. Someone had to remember what was due a guest in the house! And I didn't see you resisting too strenuously!" In her anger she had forgotten the precariousness of her situation and had risen slightly in the water. Marcos's sudden silence recalled her attention to her vulnerable position. With a cry of dismay she grabbed a washcloth and held it to her wet, heaving breasts.

"Do you know," Marcos drawled, "I do believe we are having our first lovers' quarrel."

"We aren't lovers!"

"No, not yet," he agreed tersely, his eyes devouring her wet, glistening skin.

"Not ever!" she denied hotly, flushing to the roots of her damp hair.

"We will leave that discussion for a later time. I have something else on my mind right now, and when the time comes to discuss our . . . relationship, I want to give you my complete and undivided attention."

The note of passion in his voice made her tremble, and fatalistically she wondered how she would ever resist him if he ever did put his whole efforts into seducing her.

"But now we must talk," he continued. "Here. Get out and come into the bedroom. I can't carry on a rational conversation with you like this. The bubbles are starting to dissolve!"

"Well, I didn't invite you in here!" Alex choked indignantly. "You just stroll in here, as if you have every right in the world . . ." Her words trailed off as his eyes widened and his lips twitched in sardonic amusement.

"And I haven't? I distinctly remember that this morning you promised quite a few rights to me."

"Marcos, please!" she cried desperately. "Will you kindly get out of here and let me dress?"

He had been on the point of leaving, but he stopped. "Are you presuming to give me orders?" he asked with dangerous softness.

For once Alex's frustration overrode her good sense, and her jaw tightened mutinously. "Yes! Out!"

"And what if I choose to stay?" Purposefully he took a step nearer.

The wicked gleam in his eye broke the tenuous hold she had been keeping on her self-control. Her volatile emotions finally got the better of her, and with a cry of rage she threw the wet washcloth and caught him squarely in the head. Slowly he removed the offending cloth, a look of blank astonishment on his face that quickly turned to smoldering rage.

"Oh, dear!" she wailed, appalled at what she had done. "I—I didn't mean to do that!"

For a moment the tense silence held her breathless, then a rare smile warmed Marcos's eyes as he read her honest consternation. "You are going to pay for that one, *chiquita*," he said softly. "I'll give you exactly two minutes to come out, and then I'm coming back after you!"

After the door closed behind him, Alex wasted precious seconds trying to regain her composure. Her heart was pounding so hard she thought it would suffocate her.

"One minute!" he called from the bedroom. Frantically she scurried out of the water and snatched up the towel. She barely did more than give her body a rapid once-over before donning her robe. She didn't have a doubt in this world that Marcos would carry out his threat.

With a scant second to spare, she dashed breathlessly into the next room. "I made it!" she announced triumphantly.

"For which I am sure you are thankful, my sweet," he drawled. "Now come to me and take your punishment. I have never before had a wet cloth thrown in my face."

"I—I said I was sorry, Marcos," she apologized nervously, very aware of her nakedness under the robe.

"Just how sorry are you?" He smiled. "Come here and show me!"

Alex swallowed hard, but she didn't dare deny him his retaliation. She had a dreadful suspicion that it would be worse for her if he were forced to come to her. With each step she took, she felt her limbs grow weaker. Her chest contracted painfully as he reached out and took her wrist, his thumb seeking her throbbing pulse. With a gasp she tried to pull her hand away, but his grip merely tightened.

"Come, Alex," he murmured softly. "Don't fight me! I am in a dangerous mood. Frustration does terrible things to a man!" His eyes glittered dangerously as he slowly pulled her into his arms.

"Marcos, please!" she begged.

"Marcos, please. Marcos, please. Is that all you can say? Well, you deny me my rights as your husband, but at least you can offer me a little comfort and consolation."

The intensity of his words sent a thrill through her veins. Her husband! Her breathing became heavy as for a moment he held her close, savoring her nearness. She felt so small and frail in his strong arms.

"Your hair is wet," he murmured, but that didn't prevent him from rubbing his cheek slowly against it. "What is that scent you use?"

"It—it's jasmine," she whispered against his shoulder. He hadn't dressed for dinner yet, and his casual shirt was open nearly to his waist. The soft hair on his chest curled against her throat where the deep V of her robe left her skin exposed.

"Oh, I needed this!" he muttered almost to himself, and with a groan he brought his lips down on hers in a hard, punishing kiss that robbed her of all coherent thought. She was barely aware of his fingers at her waist loosening the tie until she felt cool air on her shoulder where Marcos's hands had pulled the robe aside. His lips followed the smooth line of her jaw, trailed down her neck, and rested in the vulnerable hollow of her shoulder.

Suddenly she gave a breathless gasp. "Marcos!" she cried in pleasure-pain. His one hand had pulled apart the front of her robe and sought out the rounded fullness of her breast.

"Mmmm," he murmured against her heated skin. "So soft, so sweet!"

She scarcely heard him as she felt her nipple hardening in desire against his palm. She wanted to fight him. Her hands moved to his head, but instead of pushing him away, her traitorous fingers curled themselves into his thick hair, pulling him tighter against her as he nuzzled against her neck, inhaled the sweet fragrance of her skin, nibbled gently on her shoulder.

"You drive a man crazy!" he whispered, and he raised his head and captured her lips once again, moving his mouth on hers with a hungry urgency that demanded more and more and more.

She was lost. Her inhibitions fled as his hands became more sure, more firm. Eagerly she surrendered to the kiss, molding her body to his—half fearing, half longing for him to continue.

"No time, no time," he muttered harshly, almost incoherently, and before she could catch her breath, he moved her gently away from him, pulled the lapels of her robe together over her bare breasts, and tightened the belt. "But now we must talk!"

Alex returned to earth with a jolt. She had steeled herself for his touch, and now he left her with a curious mixture of relief and frustration.

"Are you listening, Alex?" he asked tersely, and she was chilled by the ease with which he could arouse their passion and then cool his own ardor so quickly while she remained caught in a state of emotional suspense.

"We must plan," he continued, and she forced herself to concentrate on what he was saying. "First of all, you must unlock the communicating door so we can . . . er . . . communicate easily. Where is the key?"

Reluctantly Alex opened the drawer of her nightstand and handed him the oversized key. Would he take advantage of the situation? she wondered fearfully as he fit it into the lock.

"All right, now what?" she asked, keeping her eyes averted from the open door.

A smile tugged at the corners of his mouth. "Alex, my dear, you are about to shine."

"What do you mean?" she asked weakly.

"I mean that Elena is not going to be allowed to dominate the dinner conversation. Tonight I want you to dress in your finest. You are going to be at your gayest, wittiest, and most charming. After dinner, you will play for us—all evening. And at every opportunity, we are going to demonstrate what a happy, devoted couple we are. This is our acting debut. Until Elena leaves, we are going to give every appearance of being madly in love!"

Alex was grateful that on that final pronouncement he left her to change for dinner. His words had hurt her almost unbearably. Pretend to be madly in love, when just the sight of him nearly tore her heart out! She could only pray that he didn't recognize the truth when he saw it.

With a great deal of misgiving she turned to her wardrobe to select a costume for their real-life drama. Finally she settled on a sophisticated long white sheath shot through with threads of silver. The dress was cut low both in front and in back and showed off the perfection of her figure. She had just finished applying the last of her makeup when Marcos knocked perfunctorily on the connecting door and entered without waiting for a reply. Before she could protest, he thrust a box into her lap.

"Here," he said without preamble. "I want you to pick out anything that pleases you and wear something different each evening."

Slowly Alex opened the jewelry box. Diamonds, emeralds, pearls, sapphires gleamed in the lights against the dark blue lining. Necklaces, bracelets, earrings, broaches, of a quality and size to make any woman stare.

"Marcos!" Alex whispered reverently. "I've never seen anything like this!"

"They were my mother's, but they're yours now," he announced matter-of-factly.

Alex went pale at the thought of being given a king's ransom as nonchalantly as some men would give a flower. "But—but I can't accept this!"

"You're my wife, Alex," he said coldly. "I told you in the beginning that you had a great deal to gain from this marriage."

His words chilled her, and her heart sank. How could she ever make him believe that the only thing she wanted to gain from their marriage was his love? "Very well, Marcos," she said quietly.

He watched her as she chose a diamond and

platinum necklace, but as she raised her hands to fasten it around her neck he took it from her. "Allow me."

His fingers were warm against her skin as he hooked the clasp and reached around to settle the necklace on her throat. Try as she might, she couldn't suppress the involuntary shiver that his intimate touch produced. His eyes met hers in the mirror in mute question.

"It's cold," she offered lamely and knew by the sardonic smile that curved his lips that she didn't fool him for a minute.

"Then let me warm you," he said softly as he drew her unresistingly to her feet.

"Marcos, please!" she groaned as he placed his lips against the side of her neck.

"Yes," he breathed against her ear, deliberately misunderstanding her. "I like it when a woman begs me."

His arms around her were too firm to permit a struggle, but she doubted that she could have resisted him in any case as his mouth found hers. Their earlier encounter had left her vulnerable and susceptible to his touch. He raised the process of arousal to an art, and she was powerless to deny him what he wanted as he molded her body to his and slipped one hand into the deep V of her neckline with a new possessiveness. He teased and caressed the soft flesh until her breasts hardened with desire and the nipples stood out taut against the fabric of her gown. His other hand left a trail of fire down her back, and she moaned with pleasure, her body trembling with longing as she abandoned herself to his lovemaking. His lips claimed hers with a treacherous ease, and it didn't seem possible to her that he felt nothing of what his kiss and touch implied. But even as the hope was raised in her, his next words cast her into despair.

"There!" he stated with satisfaction as he lifted his head and looked down into her dazed eyes. "That is just the expression I want Elena to see. No, don't smooth your hair. I want you to look well loved."

For a moment Alex thought that the pain was going to tear her apart. How could any man be so callous and unfeeling? Defiantly she shook off his arm that had been around her waist.

"Then, by all means, let's go down," she said on a shuddering breath. "We wouldn't want your efforts to be wasted!"

He caught her hand again just before they entered the sitting room. Sophie and Elena were already waiting for their arrival, and the younger woman's quick gaze missed nothing of Alex's flushed cheeks and trembling lips.

"Sorry to keep you waiting," Marcos apologized airily. "Alex and I were . . . ah . . . occupied and lost track of time."

A soft chuckle came from Sophie, but Elena's lips tightened into a thin, unattractive line. Her dark eyes roved appraisingly over Alex's dress and came to rest on the diamond necklace that encircled her throat. Her indrawn breath was audible. Sophie's eyes had followed Elena's, but hers was a sigh of satisfaction.

"Ah, Marcos! You have given Alex the Rivera diamonds! Duarte, Marcos's father, had them reset for Marianna. They date back to the sixteenth century!"

"Come, *Madre*," Elena interjected sharply. "Surely Alex isn't interested in ancient history!"

A flush of confusion rose in Sophie's cheeks, and as she meekly accepted her daughter-in-law's rebuke Alex found her temper rising. "Nonsense, Elena!" She sat on the sofa by Sophie and took her hand in a warm clasp. "You know I would love to hear anything you have to say about Marcos's mother and father. I'll always regret that I never had a chance to know them." She didn't need to look at Marcos to know that she had earned his warm approval. "Sophie, Marcos has given me the whole family collection. Tomorrow you must go through it and tell me about each piece." She turned a bright, meaningless smile on Elena. "And you're welcome to join us, if you'd like, Elena. I'm sure you must have longed to handle them yourself!"

This was bringing the war to the enemy camp with a vengeance! But Elena's look of hostile loathing afforded her nothing but pleasure.

Mindful of her instructions, throughout dinner Alex did her best to monopolize the conversation, abetted by Marcos's gentle promptings. She was hard put, however, to come up with amusing anecdotes about her travels without revealing to Marcos the nature of her work abroad, and it was forcibly brought home to her what an essentially uneventful life she had lived.

Halfway through the main course her invention flagged, and Elena would have jumped into the breach if Marcos hadn't intervened with a story of his own. By the time coffee was served, Elena sat stiff and silent in her chair, twin spots of color high on her cheeks. Sophie had been delighted with Marcos's unusual animation and had listened to him with increasing enjoyment. For once she had failed to notice her daughter-in-law's mood, and Elena was laboring under the double chagrin of being both silenced and ignored.

Only when Marcos's attention had been diverted by Tomás did Sophie happen to look at Elena. "Why, my dear," she said softly, "are you feeling all right? You look quite flushed."

"I'm just a little warm, *Madre,*" she replied coldly. "It is nothing that a walk in the cool air won't cure." And she looked expectantly at Marcos, but no offer from him came. Instead he volunteered:

"I know just what you need. We will have our coffee in the music room. Perhaps we can persuade Alex to play for us."

"Ah, my dear ones," Sophie exclaimed, once again missing Elena's barely stifled protest, "nothing would please me more! Many is the time, Alex, that Marcos has entertained us on his visits to the *hacienda*."

In the face of her enthusiasm, Elena had no choice but to follow the small party to the music room.

"Is there anything special you would like to hear?" Alex asked as she seated herself at the piano.

"My aunt is a romantic like yourself," Marcos said caressingly. "Chopin, I think." And he stooped to press a lingering kiss on her upturned lips.

"Oh, Marcos!" Sophie exclaimed happily as he took a place at her side. "I can't tell you how it does my heart good to see you so content!"

As the music swelled from beneath Alex's fingers Sophie's smile of pleasure deepened while Elena's heart was filled with impotent rage, as though Alex's obvious talent were in some way a personal affront to her. Not until the clock struck eleven did she lift her hands from the keys and smile at the company—that dreamy smile she always had after playing. Marcos was quickly by her side.

"Well done, my dear," he murmured with such warmth that Alex trembled. It suddenly occurred to her that it was only when she played for him that a complete rapport existed between them, and as he left to accompany

Sophie to her room she was struck with the unpalatable thought that perhaps she was doomed to be appreciated by men for her talent alone. Her own father had valued her company for no other reason. Was there something lacking in her, or had her whole personality been so subjugated to her music that beyond her talent she was nothing?

For the first time in her life, she resented her gift. Oh, why couldn't she have been born just a nice, normal girl with all the usual girl's hopes and aspirations? Then, perhaps, Marcos could have loved her in the natural course of things. As quickly as the idea entered her head, she rejected it. If it hadn't been for her talent, she and Marcos would have never met. And she would have never loved, never despaired. . . .

Alex was so engrossed in her own thoughts that she had forgotten Elena was in the room until a snort of irritation reached her. It took a moment for her eyes to lose the inner vision and focus on the sleek perfection of Elena Ortega as she sat drumming her fingers against the back of a chair.

"You think you are so smart, don't you?" Elena spat.

Refusing to be drawn, Alex rose and moved to go past her. "I'll say good night now, Elena."

Quickly Elena's clawlike hand reached out and grabbed her. Her fingers tightened until her long red nails bit into Alex's arm. "Oh, such airs!" she snapped. "You with your diamonds and your music! You are nothing but a—"

"That's enough, Elena!" Alex cut her off. "I'm not going to quarrel with you. I'm afraid I don't go in for cat fights!"

With a cry of rage Elena pushed her away, and she staggered, only keeping herself from falling by catching hold of the back of a chair.

"You don't imagine for a moment that you are going to keep him, do you?" Elena snarled, advancing on her with a feline grace. "He's mine. He always was and he always will be!"

Alex gave an inward sigh of resignation. Short of bulldozing her way past the woman and making an undignified bolt for the door, there was nothing she could do to avoid the impending confrontation. For a moment the two women studied each other, both with obvious distaste. "You're speaking of *my husband,* Elena," Alex offered at last.

"I don't know how, but you tricked him into marriage." For the first time Alex read honest bewilderment in her eyes. "I love him. I have loved him since I was a girl."

Any sympathy or compassion Alex might have felt fled as she thought of Marcos's crippled hand. "You certainly have a strange way of showing your love," she replied coldly.

For a brief instant Elena looked taken aback. She examined Alex's face narrowly and read the open disdain there. "What— what do you mean?" she stammered.

"What do you think I mean?" Alex countered contemptuously.

"Ah, Paris. So he told you."

"Of course. I am his wife."

"But not for long," Elena cried belligerently. "You don't understand the Latin temperament if you think for a moment that our quarrels meant anything. We hate one minute and love the next, and Marcos and I would have made up our differences if you had not interfered. And once you are gone," she continued confidently, "we shall soon be reconciled."

"Forgive me if I'm not impressed by your particular brand of devotion," Alex drawled.

"Why did you do it?" she asked after a pause to still her rising anger. "His hand, I mean. What did you hope to gain?"

Elena shrugged. "Marcos has never been willing to accept the fact that he has responsibilities that he cannot just ignore. He is his father's son. He was born to be *haciendo* and rule his land and his people. What I did was for his own good, in the best interests of his family and himself!"

Her callousness, her conceit, not to mention her lack of morals, both shocked and disgusted Alex. "And in your best interest, too, of course," Alex said dryly.

"Yes, mine! I have already told you that we loved one another. I—I made a terrible mistake when I married Ramón. Poor Ramón. . . ." She made a play of dabbing her eyes with her handkerchief. "I could never be the kind of wife he wanted, and he always suspected that Marcos held my heart."

Alex was being treated to a rare performance, but she wasn't deceived for a moment. Even without Marcos's confidences, she would have known after five minutes in this woman's company that she had no heart. "Too bad for you that Marcos didn't share your . . . love," she drawled.

"I tell you he did!" Elena snapped. "We—we were lovers, but we quarreled, and when he left the *hacienda,* fool that I was, I married Ramón. I will never forgive myself for not being more patient."

That Alex could believe, but for the other, instinct and her growing knowledge of Marcos told her that unless he had changed greatly, not even as a young man would he have allowed himself to be entangled in an affair with a young cousin under his family's protection. He had too much inbred honor to indulge in anything so sordid.

"After Ramón died," Elena continued, "we became lovers again. He took me with him everywhere. I tried to make him see that his music was nothing but the childish desire to fulfill a young boy's fantasy of fame and adulation. I pleaded with him to return to the *hacienda* and assume a man's responsibilities, but he refused to listen to reason." She shrugged casually. "So I took matters into my own hands. He is still angry with me, but soon he will return to his home and thank me for what I did."

White-faced, Alex studied the woman with wide, incredulous eyes. Elena actually believed what she was saying! Alex's hands tightened into two very unladylike fists, and it was all she could do to stifle the outraged retort that came to her lips. Elena saw the naked emotion but misinterpreted its cause.

"You must see that it is impossible for me to be reconciled to your marriage knowing that Marcos will soon regret the terrible mistake he has made. He does not love you! What hope for happiness do you have with a man who loves another woman?"

She spoke with such assurance that Alex might have been fooled into believing her if it hadn't been for the hard, calculating look in her eyes. Quickly she suppressed her anger and decided to try a little guile of her own.

"Oh, Elena, I can't tell you how I appreciate your frankness with me," she said. "You've explained so much that I haven't understood before. I can see now that your only concern has been for Marcos's future happiness."

For all her cunning. Elena was not astute when it came to other people. Still, it was fortunate for Alex that Elena was not looking into her eyes and thus missed the sardonic light that gleamed there as she continued. "But let me set your mind at rest and assure you that Marcos and I are very happy together. We share so many common interests. I'm afraid that it's too late to live in the past. We all have to look to the future, and I hope it will be some consolation to you to know that I love Marcos very much and will do everything in my power to make him happy."

Alex had not meant to bare her heart to Elena, but when she spoke of her love for Marcos, all the intensity of her real feeling revealed itself in every line of her body, every note in her voice, and even Elena could not help but be struck by the throbbing sincerity in her words.

"But—but we were lovers!" she sputtered.

"Whatever he felt for you will soon be forgotten," Alex assured her kindly.

"I tell you he loves me!" Elena insisted desperately.

"Of course he does," Alex replied soothingly. "You are his cousin, the companion of his youth, the object of his boyhood infatuation."

"And I say he is still my lover!" she cried.

"We're both women enough to know that old habits die hard." Alex nodded wisely. "You are like an old, comfortable slipper that he was reluctant to part with."

Alex had to lift a hand to her lips to cover her smile at Elena's gasp of murderous outrage.

"Old slipper!" Elena moved so close that Alex could feel the waves of hatred emanating from the woman. Reprieve came unexpectedly from Marcos, standing in the doorway.

"Sorry to be gone so long, *querida*," he said, nonchalantly strolling into the room and stepping neatly between the two women. Alex's knees went suddenly weak and she sank against his chest. His hand under her chin forced her head up, and as their eyes met she read humor, puzzlement, and something else there that set her pulses racing.

How long had he been in the doorway? she wondered wildly. How much had he heard of the conversation?

"Ready for bed, *mi amor*?" he said caressingly, ignoring his cousin's presence, and with a cry of rage Elena flung out of the room, slamming the door behind her. But Alex scarcely noticed. Her eyes were still drowning in Marcos's deep green pools.

Then he pushed her slightly away and cocked one sardonic eyebrow at her. His lips twitched until a full smile revealed the neat, even row of his white teeth, and, to Alex's astonishment, he threw back his head and laughed the most spontaneous laugh she had ever heard from him.

"Marcos?" she asked hesitantly.

He pulled her close once again, and just before his lips found hers, she heard him laugh. "Old slipper?"

Chapter Nine

$\mathcal{A}$ week after her confrontation with Elena, Alex received her second early-morning visit from Marcos. On this occasion he didn't bother to knock, but since she was still blissfully asleep, she wasn't in any condition to protest his free use of the connecting door. As he had done before, he watched her a moment, but this time a faint smile played around the corners of his mouth. The bed dipped as he knelt on the edge with one knee, and then, supporting himself with his hands on either side of her sleeping form, he leaned over and placed a gentle kiss on her parted lips. Just for a moment she responded before her eyes opened, but her cry of alarm was smothered by his hard, firm mouth.

Her hands came up to push him away, but as they met the soft mat of curly hair on his chest, exposed by his open shirt, they weakly withdrew. Marcos took this opportunity to rest himself against her soft breasts, holding her in place by the weight of his body.

"Good morning," he whispered softly when

he had left her too dazed to resist him. "Now that's what I call the proper way to start the day."

"What—what are you doing here?" she stammered, breathless.

"Nothing to cause you alarm." He smiled. "If it will ease your mind, I'll tell you that Tomás has breakfast waiting for me. I just came in to tell you that I had a call late last night and I must leave for Tepic within the hour."

Much too aware of the pleasurable sensation the feel of his body was arousing in her, she squirmed under him, and to her shame she was disappointed when he obligingly sat up. Fighting down such dangerous thoughts, she hoisted herself higher on the pillows and tucked the sheet firmly under her chin.

"You—you're going into Tepic?" she repeated. "Alone?"

"Did you think I was going to invite Elena to go along?" he drawled, raising one ironic eyebrow.

"No! I guess I was just having a lovely vision of being able to escape for a day myself. That's out of the question, I suppose," she added gloomily.

"I'm sorry, my dear. I'm afraid it is, but I'll be back this evening. Don't wait dinner for me, though. I suspect it will be a long session. You'll be all right here?"

She noted the trace of anxiety in his eyes and forced a smile to her lips. "Are you afraid

Elena will knife me in the back while you're gone? Don't worry. I'll be careful."

"And I will ask Tomás to keep an eye on you," he said grimly.

"Do—do you have to go?" she asked diffidently.

"My, my! I think I should be flattered by this sudden desire for my company. I've had the distinct impression these past few days that you've been avoiding me."

He was right, but Alex hadn't realized he'd noticed. In the past week, she was aware of both obvious and more subtle changes in him that had surprised and intrigued her but at the same time had made her uneasy and nervous in his company. Much of his former tension was gone, and he seemed much more likely to smile than frown, but there was a certain recklessness about him. His eyes as they rested on Elena had lost much of their frustrated rage. If anything, they held only mild annoyance or complete indifference. As his anger faded, the lines of bitterness around his mouth and nose softened until Alex could only describe his whole expression as mellow.

What troubled her was his attitude toward herself, which had also undergone a change. Often she found his eyes following her with a strange, disturbing expression that was a mixture of assessment and calculation. He no longer snapped at her or engaged her in his subtle battle of wills, but neither did he make any effort to pursue her. If she had to give his attitude a name, she would call it waiting and expectant, and she found it easier if she just stayed out of his way.

"Well?" he broke into her thoughts.

"Well, what?" she prevaricated.

"Well, will you really be sorry to have me gone today?"

"I . . . I . . ." she stammered, for the life of her unable to answer. She didn't know how she felt!

"Never mind!" He frowned, levering himself off the bed. "Don't put your immortal soul in jeopardy with a lie. Give Sophie my regards."

A lump rose in Alex's throat as she watched him leave. She had the uncomfortable sensation that she had disappointed him, though just what he had expected from her she didn't know. With a sigh, she pushed aside the covers and reached for her robe. Sleep was out of the question, though it was only a little after seven. Perhaps a swim would clear her confused mind and give her the courage to face the day ahead.

For the past week she had exerted herself to keep Elena entertained so that Marcos would be left free to work. The problem was that Elena, it seemed, never exposed her delicate skin to the aging sunlight or the drying effects of salt water, which meant the beach was out. She never read, nor was she interested in exploring the markets in San Blas. Most of the time she spent prowling around the room, listening for the sounds of Marcos's arrival.

Sophie was no problem at all, Alex thought fondly. She was perfectly content to attend to her embroidering, carrying on a rambling conversation as she bent over her work. Alex had enjoyed listening to her reminisce about her past—the sheltered, protected life she had lived as a girl.

Afternoons, Alex was able to escape to the music room while the women took their traditional siestas. At least she could look forward to her afternoons being profitably filled. But soon that relief would be at an end. Marcos had finished the last movement of the *Night Suite* two days before, and now they were polishing the work. She didn't know just how much of that he had in mind, but it couldn't take a day or two more at most. As long as Sophie and Elena remained, she knew Marcos would want her to stay, but then what? She longed to know what his plans were next, but she didn't ask the question—because she dreaded to hear the answer. Her position was too insecure. He only had to speak the word and she would be sent into exile.

The morning turned out to be even worse than she had anticipated. Cowardly, she put off telling Elena and Sophie about Marcos's absence as long as possible. By midmorning she couldn't procrastinate any longer. Elena was nervously pacing the room, her eyes moving constantly to the door.

"Where's Marcos?" she demanded at last.

"Oh, he had to go into Tepic today. He received a call about some business he had to take care of. I'm sorry; I should have mentioned it before," she apologized. "Sophie, he sends his regards. He'll be back this evening."

Alex had expected Elena to be annoyed, but she wasn't prepared for the woman's violent reaction.

"Tepic? Why? Who called him?" she demanded.

Warily Alex watched her face first pale and then flame with color. "I really can't say, Elena—"

"You do know!" Elena's fingers bit into her shoulder. "Tell me! Why did he go, you scheming little—"

"Elena! You will apologize at once!" Sophie gasped.

It seemed for a moment that her daughter-in-law hadn't heard. Then slowly she turned dazed, frightened eyes on Sophie. "But Marcos, why has he gone?" she repeated, almost to herself.

"What Marcos chooses to do is no concern of yours, Elena," her mother-in-law said sharply. "Since when are the men in our family answerable to anyone for their actions?"

Alex couldn't wholly applaud this chauvinistic sentiment, but she was devoutly grateful for Sophie's intervention. Gradually the wild light faded from Elena's eyes, and she looked at her hand still gripping Alex's shoulder as though it belonged to another person. Then with a muttered oath—thankfully inaudible— she pushed Alex aside and stormed from the room.

Pain and bewilderment filled Sophie's eyes as she watched her departure. "I'm so sorry, Alex, my dear," she said, distractedly fingering the lace edge of her handkerchief. "I just don't know what's wrong with the girl. I've never seen her behave like this."

Alex collapsed wearily on the sofa and soothingly patted the older woman's hand. "Don't let it worry you, Sophie. I'm not offended. Elena's obviously just going through a difficult time. She's restless and a little bored."

"But it was she who urged me to come." Sophie frowned in bewilderment. "Oh, not that I haven't enjoyed every minute of our visit," she added quickly. She smiled affectionately at Alex and returned the pressure of her hand. "You must know how fond I've become of you, my dear. Though we don't see each other nearly as often as I would like, our family is close. Marcos has always been like a son to me. I would do anything for his happiness, as I know he would do for mine."

"He loves you dearly, Sophie, and it isn't hard to see why."

Sophie leaned over and placed a soft kiss

against Alex's cheek. "You are a sweet, talented young woman, Alex—just the woman Marcos deserves. And I can see that you love him very much. It is a great pleasure to welcome you to our family."

Alex was so moved by the tribute that for a moment she couldn't speak. When she had agreed to marry Marcos, she hadn't thought of it as joining a family, and now the idea brought a warmth that curled down and nestled happily in her heart. Oh, if only this belonging could be a reality! But as quickly as the hope arose, it died. What had Sophie said? Marcos would do anything for her happiness —and no one knew the truth of that better than Alex. For Sophie's peace of mind he had kept quiet about his "accident," endured Elena's presence at *Casa de Rivera,* been driven into marrying Alex herself. Sophie had spoken confidently—as well she might—about Alex's love for Marcos, but she had said nothing about his returning that love. And there was the crux of the problem, she thought despondently.

Sophie and Alex were spared Elena's presence for the remainder of the day. She sent word that she had a headache and thankfully didn't put in an appearance until dinnertime. As she took her place at the table Alex noted with alarm that, while she was outwardly composed, she showed signs of an inner agitation. All her makeup couldn't conceal the unnatural pallor and the dark circles under her eyes. A muscle beside her full red mouth twitched uncontrollably, and when she helped herself to the tray of meat Tomás held for her, her hands trembled noticeably. Obviously her nerves were strung almost to the breaking point. Something more than frustration at Marcos's absence and boredom was troubling her, and for the first time Alex wondered if the woman was on the verge of a breakdown. Was it possible that she loved Marcos deeply enough to become emotionally disturbed by his rejection?

Dinner was a silent meal. Elena's attitude toward Alex was decidedly glacial, and Alex sighed in relief when Tomás removed the last of the dishes. "Shall we have coffee in the sitting room?" she asked brightly with a determined cheerfulness.

Fortunately for the state of her own nerves, she had barely poured the coffee when Marcos strolled casually into the room.

"Marcos!" She sighed thankfully.

With the arrival of her nephew, Sophie's body visibly relaxed and her eyes shone with patent relief. To Alex's surprise, Elena neither moved nor spoke. She had expected the woman to greet him with even more than her usual effusiveness, but instead her dark gaze remained fixed on his face, her face pale.

Marcos took in the situation at a glance as he saw Alex's and Sophie's relieved expressions. Casually he crossed to Alex and kissed her gently on her upturned lips, his eyes mocking but not unkind as he drawled, "Have you had a good day?"

Her own twisted smile spoke volumes.

"And how was your day, my dear?" his aunt asked, lifting her cheek for his kiss.

"Very interesting," he answered vaguely. "And how about you, Elena? Have you managed to keep yourself occupied?" He took a chair across from her where he could watch the changing emotions that played over her face.

"Where have you been?" Elena demanded, her voice strained.

"Why, didn't Alex tell you?" His eyebrows raised in mock surprise "I had business in Tepic."

Elena waved away his answer with an impatient hand. "Yes, yes. But where? With whom?"

"My, you are persistent, aren't you?" he drawled. "Well, if you must know, Sánchez flew in from Mexico City to see me."

"Your lawyer?" Sophie interjected. "Is anything wrong?"

"Oh, nothing I can't handle," he replied enigmatically, his eyes never leaving Elena's face. "But what have you been up to, Elena?" When she didn't answer, he continued casually enough but with an irony that didn't escape Alex. "You're looking pale, my dear cousin. I'm afraid that our quiet way of life is beginning to annoy you. Perhaps you think your time could be more profitably spent."

What was Marcos up to? Alex wondered. He was obviously taunting Elena, but his innuendoes meant nothing to herself. Curiously she studied his face. His expression was deliberately blank, but his eyes betrayed a suppressed anger. Sophie, too, was gazing at him in puzzlement. Only Elena seemed to find meaning in his words. Her eyes darkened ominously, and the twitch beside her mouth became even more pronounced.

"Shall we have a little chat," he persisted, "and see what we can do to provide better for your entertainment?"

Alex expected Elena to jump at this opportunity to get Marcos to herself, but instead she shrank bank in her chair, a flush rising in her neck to her ears.

"You must be missing your travels, hmmm?" Marcos continued. "I understand you recently spent some time in Acapulco. I realize that San Blas can't compete for amusement, but then perhaps what you need most is a nice long rest. Isn't that right?"

Growing more and more curious at this strange exchange, Alex looked from Elena to Marcos and back again. His jaw had tightened. Elena swallowed hard and licked her lips to moisten them. In her eyes was the fear of a cornered animal. For once even Sophie was aware of the undercurrents.

"Isn't that right, Elena?" he repeated grimly.

"Yes . . . no! I don't know!" she cried, driven. "Oh, why didn't you return to the *hacienda!* Why did you marry that—"

"Elena! We will have no more of that talk!" Sophie's voice held a new sternness that her daughter-in-law couldn't ignore. "You are right, Marcos. I think Elena needs to return home and rest. She is not herself." She forced a smile to her lips. "And what about you? Perhaps a time of rest on the *hacienda* would do you good, also."

"I'm afraid Alex and I have other commitments," he said gently. "And I've made arrangements for the builders to begin work restoring the central portion of the house. You see, Alex likes it here. Rustic, I think you called it, didn't you, my dear?"

These were the first words he had addressed directly to her since his greeting, and it took her a minute to respond.

"Yes, rustic," she repeated mechanically, unsure what he expected from her.

"You can't mean to stay here!" Elena suddenly interrupted, desperation in her words. "You must return to the *hacienda!* I—we need you!"

"I know just how you need me, my dear cousin," he said sharply, "and apparently I don't have to return for that! Besides," he added deliberately, "my work is here."

"Work? What work? You were born to be *haciendo!* You cannot mean to waste your life in idleness," she cried scornfully.

"I have no intention of being idle!" He cocked one eyebrow at Alex. "Do you think it is time we let Sophie and Elena in on our little secret?"

This confirmed what Alex had suspected: Marcos considered the work on *Night Suite* completed. Obviously Elena, too, would be gone, and he would no longer need her. Her heart contracted painfully, but she answered quietly, "Yes, of course."

"What secret?" Elena seemed to be recovering some of her composure, and the stridency was back in her voice.

"Come. We'll show you."

Sophie rose quickly, Elena more reluctantly, as Marcos stood to usher them out the door. "The music room, please."

"Sit down, Elena, Sophie," he said a few moments later. "You must forgive me for not sharing my secret with you from the beginning, but I wanted to wait until the work was finished."

"What work?" Elena repeated in frustration.

"You know that my days of performing are over," he said dryly but without his usual bitterness. "But with Alex's help I do not have to forsake my music entirely. I have turned my hand to composition, and I've just finished my first major work. You shall have the privilege—or should I say duty?" he amended, smiling, "—of being the first to hear it. Alex, if you please?"

He motioned her to the piano, and she saw that both the *Mexican Rhapsody* and the *Night Suite* were gathered together and waiting on the music rest.

"I think perhaps the rhapsody first and then the suite," he suggested taking his place in his usual chair.

As he leaned back, Elena shifted forward, her eyes focused on the handwritten manuscript. Acutely aware of the waves of hostility from across the room, Alex's hands shook slightly as she arranged the pages. She took a deep breath and tried to detach her thoughts from the palpable tensions and concentrate on the music before her.

"Well," Elena snapped waspishly, "how long do we have to wait to hear this masterpiece?"

"Relax, Alex," Marcos said sharply, and a lifetime of training and discipline responded to the command. With a sureness and precision that surprised even her, she began, and as always, once immersed in the music, her thoughts transcended her surroundings.

For a full minute after she brought her hands crashing down on the final chords of the suite, silence prevailed. Tears ran unashamedly down Sophie's face. Marcos sat with his head back against the chair, his eyes bright slits under his lowered lashes. Elena's presence brought the only discordant note to the room. Her face was filled with such anger and loathing that Alex didn't think it possible for her to contain it long.

She was right. The eruption, when it occurred, took only Sophie by surprise. With a cry of rage Elena jumped from her chair, her hands clenching and unclenching at her sides, and all her anger was directed at Alex. For a moment she thought Elena would spring at her, but in an instant Marcos stood between them.

"You see, Elena. I have found my life's work."

"Oh, it was wonderful, wonderful!" Sophie exclaimed, dabbing at her wet cheeks.

Wildly Elena looked from Sophie to Alex to Marcos, and a shudder vibrated through her body. "You—you never mean to return to the *hacienda*, do you!"

"No, Elena. I don't—not in the way you would have. I told you so years ago, but you refused to accept it. Now you must if you are to have any peace."

"Peace! I don't want peace!" she cried, her face pale and drawn.

"At the moment, I don't think you know what you want. Go to bed now," he said wearily, a look of something approaching compassion in his eyes. "You are overtired."

"I don't want your pity, damn you!"

"No more tonight! You are upsetting Sophie," he said firmly, turning her toward the door. "We will discuss your plans tomorrow."

With a sob of rage and frustration Elena shook off his hand and without a backward glance ran from the room.

"Oh, Marcos!" Sophie wailed. "What is wrong with the child? I am so worried about her. What am I going to do?"

"Nothing," he said gently. "Leave it to me. She needs to settle down, Sophie, in a place of her own. I don't think the *hacienda* is good for her. An apartment in Mexico City would suit her well. There she could make friends, and I know you will not be hurt if I say she needs to consider a second marriage. She loved Ramón deeply, of course," he added, not quite meeting his aunt's eyes, "but she is too young to mourn forever, and she has no child to bring her comfort as you had. We must be unselfish in this, Sophie, and allow her to make a new life."

Wearily Sophie ran a hand over her eyes. "Yes, yes. You know, Marcos, that I once hoped you and she . . . Ah, forgive me, Alex. I love you dearly. I just felt that Marcos was the person who could have tamed the wildness in her, but I could not wish him a better wife than you."

"Go to bed now, Sophie," he urged gently.

"And don't worry about Elena. She will listen to me. You know that I will do only what is best for us all."

With that Sophie had to be satisfied, and indeed, Alex saw the lines of anxiety fade. Her trust in Marcos was absolute.

"Good night, then, my dears." She rose to place a kiss on Alex's cheek. "Yes, *niña*," she said sweetly, "you do our family proud."

Chapter Ten

As Sophie's footsteps faded down the hallway Alex sat at the piano, emotionally spent.
Slowly Marcos turned and held out his hand
to her, his eyes glowing with a new softness.

"Sophie is right, Alex. You do our family
proud."

Though he touched her with nothing but his
gaze, Alex was drawn to him like metal to a
magnet. As if in a dream, she rose and moved
into his arms, desperately needing the comfort and solace of his embrace. His lips and
hands were gentle as he smoothed her hair
away from her forehead and kissed the corners of her mouth, the smooth line of her
cheek, and finally her soft, welcoming lips.
Alex knew it was dangerous. The events of the
day had left her weak and vulnerable to his
caress, the hard security of his arms. What
did it matter if he didn't love her? she thought
dizzily. At least at this moment he offered her
escape, protection, respite from the ugly
world.

He could not help but be aware of her vulnerability, and he took full advantage of it. His hands moved possessively over her shoulders and back. His mouth, at first gentle and caressing, hardened, and comfort gave way to a growing need within her for more and more of what he offered. Contentment dissolved with her rising desire, and under the insistent pressure of his hands and lips she knew again the vague frustration that had so disturbed her before.

She strained against his body and felt his growing desire for her. To know that his need equaled her own was nearly her undoing, and she fought against the temptation to surrender herself to a passion she knew could consume her.

"Alex?" He breathed against her lips—and desire trembled down the length of his body.

"No!" she protested weakly.

Slowly he released her, and perversely she would have felt forsaken if it hadn't been for the burning glow in his eyes as they devoured her face then settled on her mouth, red and swollen from his kiss and still pulsing with desire. His hand trembled slightly as he cupped her cheek, and only half aware of what she was doing, she turned her face to press her lips against his palm.

Gently he pulled her head against his chest and stroked her hair, his fingers soothing and calming her now until her heart slowed its rapid beat, her breathing became deep and regular—and she was at peace.

"Are you too tired to go for a swim?" he asked.

She felt his voice husky and deep against her cheek, and she raised her head to gaze into his face. She knew what impulse motivated him. She, too, would welcome a chance to relax and wash away the bitterness of the day in the warm water of the sea.

"Go and change," he said, reading the acquiescence in her eyes. "I'll meet you in ten minutes."

Marcos was waiting for her in the sitting room when she rejoined him. A towel robe was thrown carelessly around his shoulders, revealing his chest and the fine dark hair that formed a triangle down to where it met his brief bathing trunks. Just the sight of him sent her senses leaping, and when he smiled, the force of his personality left her weak.

The weeks of rest and good food had added flesh to her bones, and Marcos's eyes traveled caressingly over her nicely rounded curves revealed by her bikini. She wished that she had chosen a less revealing suit, but in her haste she had just grabbed the first one at hand.

"Come, *mi amor!*" Marcos murmured.

Alex felt a quiver of anticipation as hand in hand they slipped out the patio door and down the path. The fragrance of wisteria and gardenia washed over her like a balm. In this world of lush sweetness outside, it was hard to believe that anger, hatred, and heartbreak could exist, Alex though dreamily. Oh, how she had come to love San Blas!

The sand was still warm under their feet as they made their way across the beach to the water. For a long moment they stood silent, just letting the foam swirl around their ankles as it ebbed and flowed. The inevitable breaking of the waves against the shore was infinitely soothing.

Marcos stood close beside her, but not touching her now. The tension in her, however, began to build as she felt his eyes examining her face. "Do—do you come out often at night?" she asked lightly to break the silence.

"More often this past week than ever before," he replied dryly. "I find that a swim has a soothing effect when I've become . . . er . . . overstimulated during the day."

Alex blushed in confusion, very aware of the implication in his words, but before she had time to withdraw mentally from him, he continued impersonally. "Look at the water. The phosphorus in the moonlight makes it look like a fairyland. As a child growing up in the city, did you ever dream of a place like this?"

"I—I never had much time to dream," she said hesitantly, unconsciously echoing her words to Pieter.

"Of course," he said wryly, "you were too busy at the piano. You made your own magic instead of seeking it in the outside world. I wonder if that will always be enough for you," he mused, and Alex caught a seriousness behind his words. "I could show you that there are many other pleasures to be found beyond your music, *querida*—if you would let me." And he reached out a hand and ran his fingers caressingly down her bare arm.

The moonlight, the water, the night sounds, his touch—suddenly they were too much for her to bear. With a strangled sound, she jerked away from him.

"You should not do that, *chiquita*," he said softly. "After a day filled with emotion, I have little self-control left, and when you resist me, you bring out the hunter in me and make me forget all my honorable intentions."

In the moonlight his eyes were dark and unfathomable, but his aura of masculine virility reached out to her like an enveloping cloak. If she didn't escape, her will to resist him would be gone. With a cry she ran into the sea until the water was deep enough to allow her to swim. She didn't have to look to know that he was right behind her, but he made no attempt to touch her again, merely catching up with her and matching his strokes to hers.

Side by side they swam until they reached the line of breakers. Then together they turned and rode the waves back in to shore.

They didn't speak, and it wasn't until the third time out that Marcos reached out one lazy hand and caught her outstretched arm. She lost her balance and foundered, but Marcos had her secure, and she was powerless to stop him as he pulled her close. His cool, wet lips found hers with unerring accuracy. His legs entwined with hers, and down, down they went into the dark sea.

Alex's whole body was alive with sensations —the feel of Marcos's warm body, the caress of the cooler water, the pressure of his lips. When they struck the sandy bottom, he gave a push that quickly propelled them upward, never once breaking the embrace. Only when they surfaced did he lift his mouth, allowing her to catch her breath. His hands encircled her waist lightly as they trod water. With a burst of energy she broke away from him and swam quickly toward shore. To her relief, he made no attempt to catch her.

If she could just hide from him a moment, she thought frantically, until her own traitorous body had a chance to recover from the sensual arousal in the water.

As soon as her feet touched sand, she rose and began to run along the wet beach. A quick glance over her shoulder warned her that Marcos was following, but his pace was slow, even casual. On and on she ran, leaving him well behind, until she came to a small outcropping of rock large enough to hide herself.

She crouched behind it, closing her eyes and leaning her cheek against its rough surface as she gasped for breath.

The sound of the surf deadened his approach, and it wasn't until his amused laugh came to her from just above her head that she realized she had been discovered.

"Quite useless to try and hide, *mi amor*," he observed dryly. "Look at yourself."

For several seconds she didn't understand, but then, as she slowly opened her eyes and looked up at him, she saw what he meant. He stood legs apart, hands on his hips, and her eyes were drawn instantly to his briefs. The phosphorus from the sea clung to the wet fabric, making it glow. A quick glance down at herself revealed the worst. She, too, was glittering with the same eerie light. Marcos couldn't have missed seeing her! No wonder he had allowed her to escape, she thought bitterly.

As she would have risen, his hands caught her shoulders and forced her off balance. With a cry she tumbled onto the soft, deep sand. Before she could rise, Marcos was there, his body outstretched beside hers. "Don't fight me, Alex," he said tensely. "We've both known that this time would have to come. We've been through too much, shared too much. It was inevitable from the first time we kissed."

He held her down while his eyes roamed hungrily over her slim, lithe body, gleaming white in the moonlight. They stopped to dwell on the shadowed valley between her breasts, exposed to his gaze by the cut of her suit.

"I've never seen a woman look so beautiful," he murmured huskily as he supported himself on one elbow and let his fingers trail from her neck to her throat to the swelling curve of her breast. Her nerves quivered with the havoc his hands were creating. Oh, why couldn't she hate him? she thought bitterly. Was there no justice in the world that she should love him so while for him she was nothing but a transitory passion? Desperately she fought the wave of longing his lovemaking brought. She dug her teeth into her lower lip to withstand the onslaught as his hands wandered in tantalizing exploration over her ribs and hips and back up to her face.

"You are such an interesting contradiction, *querida*," he murmured, puzzled as his fingers traced the taut line of her mouth. "You set your mind against me when I know that your body longs to respond. What do I have to do to put your mind and body in harmony? Hmmm?"

She soon saw that his question was rhetorical as he began his attack on her with sensual ease. His breath was warm against her cheek as he nibbled gently on her exposed ear. With a sob she steeled herself against his practiced lovemaking. How many other women had he kissed in just this way? she thought wildly, trying to rouse her anger against him.

As he turned her into his arms she closed her eyes to block out the sight of his dark, cynical face, but in despair she discovered that the darkness heightened her other senses. The sound of the water pounded in her ears. The touch of his body was cool and damp from the water. The taste of his lips as they slowly claimed hers was tangy with the brine of the sea. His whole aura surrounded her, and the emotions she felt in him were wild and primitive—as pagan as the untamed jungle and roaring ocean enclosing them. Slowly but surely he was undermining her resolve. After nearly twenty-five years of almost nunlike existence, she was discovering facets of her character hitherto unsuspected. Did every woman have hidden behind her civilized façade this overpowering need to be aroused and conquered?

She felt a sudden freedom from restriction, but it wasn't until he slowly slipped the straps from her shoulders that she realized he had unfastened the top to her suit. The cool air hardened her nipples, and his hands moved to caress the smooth whiteness of her full, rounded breasts. Her body arched against him as he replaced his hand with his mouth and caught her taut nipple between his lips. Gently he teased the soft flesh until her head was spinning with mindless pleasure. A sob of delight escaped from deep in her throat as he molded and nibbled her breast, and for just a second she felt the sharp edge of his teeth.

At the same time his wonderful hands began to move on her, playing her like a beloved instrument, teasing and tantalizing her bare flesh—and she was caught up in the rhythm and music that sang through her veins at his touch. He was the master musician and she his apprentice as he taught her the beginning ways of love. Her limbs were turning to water; her arms were almost too weak to hold him.

Helplessly she moved her hands up and down the smooth skin of his back and felt the play of muscles under her fingers. She couldn't resist the impulse to touch him, to explore his hard, firm body. Her tentative touch sent a shiver of delight through him, and he surged against her, letting her know the strength of his arousal. When she hesitated to continue, he took her hand and kissed her fingers one by one.

"Such talented little hands," he murmured and pressed her palm against his chest. "Touch me!"

At his encouragement, her movements became more sure. She laced her fingers through the hair on his chest and felt the strong beat of his heart pulsing beneath. As her hand slipped lower to the smooth flesh stretched across the ribs his stomach muscles tightened, and she reveled in the intoxicating feeling of power. That she could move him even as he moved her!

Quietly he lay supine beneath her exploring

hands, but she felt the tension in him grow as her hand became more seeking, wanting to learn every inch of his hard, muscular body. His breathing became labored and irregular, and even in the moonlight she could see the cords in his neck pulse with emotion.

Finally she slipped her hands around his shoulders and lowered herself to his chest, moving sensually, with unconscious provocation, savoring the feel of the soft hair against breasts that were hard with passion. She felt the low moan start deep in his chest before he pulled her lips down to his and muffled the sound against her open mouth.

The kiss began a new fire in her, and she welcomed his warm, searching tongue, answering every movement as he explored the moist warmth of her mouth. The world revolved dizzily around her, and it took a moment before she realized that once again she was lying on her back, Marcos's body pressing her down into the soft sand.

Briefly he raised up and looked deep into her eyes. His own glowed with triumph, and a soft laughter rumbled in his throat.

"You are a whole woman now, *mi amor*," he murmured huskily. "And soon you will be *my* woman!"

She shivered with exquisite pleasure as his hands and lips began an exploration of their own until there wasn't a curve or hollow of her body that he hadn't touched with a searing fire that threatened to consume her. She was beyond conscious thought. She could only respond, and when he parted her legs and lowered himself to her, she could only sigh with profound relief and surrender herself to the pleasure of Marcos's demanding body.

The unaccustomed weight of Marcos's arm flung carelessly around her brought Alex back from the golden world of her dreams. Gradually her eyes opened, but her bed was the soft sand, her ceiling the sky, her walls nothing but the limitless expanse of sea, her covering Marcos's robe thrown lightly over them. As memory returned she turned her head on the pillow of sand and looked at Marcos's face so close to her own. In sleep, with his hair tousled and the hard line of his jaw relaxed, he looked young and happy as she had never seen him. Fulfillment had smoothed away the lines beside his nose and curved his lips into a soft smile. Satisfaction had soothed his taut nerves, so that his body was relaxed and pliant as it stretched out beside her.

The casual possessiveness of his arm across her breasts brought a wave of color to her face, and she was torn between embarrassment and amazement as she remembered her own abandoned response to his lovemaking. She wanted to hate him—but she couldn't. Mindful of her innocence, Marcos had wooed her body into acquiescence, never forcing, never rushing, and he had finally possessed her with a patience and concern that made her pain fleeting and scarcely remembered. Gently but surely he had led her to the brink of sexual fulfillment until at last she had cried out for release, and he had taken her with an expertise that brought her the ultimate pleasure of shared intimacy.

A sigh, barely audible, escaped her lips, and Marcos's arm tightened around her for a moment. Then he turned in his sleep, and she was free from his disturbing touch.

Peace for her was impossible. Her mind was still too filled with sensual memories, vague disquiet, haunting fears. Marcos had taken her, made her physically his wife, but she had no idea whether or not this made any difference ultimately in their future. Did he still mean to send her away?

She shivered and reached for her bathing suit. Moving silently so as not to awaken Marcos, she slipped into it and made her way down to the water. She wanted to clear her mind and wash away all traces of Marcos's touch. She didn't swim out far, and as she turned, a light in the music room caught her attention. Tomás wasn't usually so careless as to leave lights on. She frowned and tried to remember. Yes, Marcos himself had turned the lights out when they had left the room.

She swam quickly back to shore, and as she stood to walk she was positive she saw a figure moving around in the room. Picking up the towel she had dropped hours before, she hurried up the path to the patio. Some instinct of trouble made her skin prickle. Should she call to Marcos. No. She wasn't prepared to face him again yet.

The door of the sitting room was ajar, and quietly she slipped in, her steps deadened by the thick carpet. Down the hall, light came from under the door of the music room. Faint sounds filtered through the heavy oak panels as she approached. Perhaps it was a prowler, and she paused for a moment, wondering if she ought to waken Tomás. Then the smell of smoke reached her.

She opened the door a crack, and at the sight that met her eyes she pushed it open wide. Kneeling on the hearth of the giant fireplace was Elena, and one by one she was feeding papers into the fire in the grate. It took Alex only a moment to realize what was happening. The piano was bare. The sheaf of papers Elena held was Marcos's manuscript. She was burning Marcos's music!

"No, no!" Alex cried in pain and rage. "Stop it!" She ran across the room and grabbed the woman by the shoulder, spinning her around. Elena was caught off balance, and with a moan she fell heavily against the stone hearth, clutching the manuscript to her. As Alex reached for it Elena's fingers found the fire poker that lay by her hand. Wildly she swung. Pain seared Alex's arm, and as she stumbled Elena rose with a cry and flung the stack of papers into the flames.

"There is your precious music!" She laughed. "See what it is worth now!"

Alex scarcely heard the words. Her one thought was to save the manuscript. Before Elena could anticipate her action, she reached into the fire and grabbed the blazing papers. With her hands she beat at the flames that curled around the edges. She couldn't save it all, but she would save most of what was left. Elena's fingernails raked her bare arm, but Alex was beyond pain. She had succeeded in putting out the last of the smoldering pages when Marcos's voice cut through the room.

"*Dios!* What is happening, Alex!"

With a cry Elena released her hold, and Alex felt Marcos lifting her gently to her feet. "Alex, what happened!"

"Oh, Marcos," she breathed on a shuddering sob, "Elena has burned your manuscript." Weakly she lay in the cirle of his arms as his eyes moved to Elena standing defiantly by the fireplace, to the charred remains of the paper on the hearth, and then to her own blackened hands. Urgently he caught her wrists and turned her palms up.

"Oh, Alex! You fool! You little fool! What have you done?"

"I—I put out the fire." She raised dazed eyes to his. "Elena would have burned it all."

"But your hands!"

She shook her head mutely, impatient with

him that he didn't realize part of his suite had been destroyed. "She had already burned some when I found her! I had to save the rest!"

"Sit down. You are in shock."

He helped her to a chair and turned to pull the bellrope. "Tomás will be here in a moment, and then we will see how much damage you have done." A movement out of the corner of his eye caught his attention. "Stay where you are, Elena! We will finish with your affairs tonight! I want you out of this house by tomorrow!"

As she shrank against the sofa a frightened Tomás burst into the room, his clothes in wild disarray. He stopped short at the sight that met his eyes, and a hysterical giggle caught in Alex's throat. What must they all look like? Two o'clock in the morning, and she and Marcos were in swimming suits. Elena sat huddled on the couch in a flaming red peignoir. The smell of smoke hung heavy in the air. And Tomás's master looked ready to tear the room apart in rage.

"Bring the first-aid kit," he ordered tersely. "And some brandy!" he added after a quick look at Alex's face.

"Marcos—" Elena began as Tomás left the room.

"*Silencio!* I have a great deal to say to you, but I will save it until I know how badly Alex is burned." He turned to Alex, shivering in her chair, and brought a soft woolen blanket from the sofa to wrap around her shoulders. "Oh, *niña!* How could you have done such a thing? Isn't it enough that Elena has destroyed my career with her malice? Must she destroy yours as well?"

The notion that the damage to her hands might prevent her from playing had never entered Alex's head, but she knew that even if she had stopped to consider the dangers involved, it wouldn't have prevented her from trying to save Marcos's music. Since she had first acknowledged her love for him, Marcos had been the most important thing in her life.

A few minutes later he wound the loose gauze over her hands to cover the ointment that he had spread so gently on her burns.

"There!" He sighed in satisfaction. "I will take you to the doctor tomorrow, but I am sure the burns are superficial."

"Do you remember the first time you administered first aid?" she said dreamily, the effects of the brandy deadening the pain and giving her world a rosy glow. "You weren't so gentle with me then."

He looked into her face and smiled. "And you weren't nearly so mellow. I seem to remember a very determined glint in your eye."

"Are you sorry I didn't just go away?"

A shuttered expression came over his face, and he turned away to replace the tubes and tape in the box. "I won't know how to answer that for a while," he replied noncommittally.

His words sobered her. For just a few moments as he had worked on her hands she had felt so close to him, and now in an instant he had again erected the barrier between them. Abruptly he moved away from her, dismissed the hovering Tomás, and turned on Elena, who had been watching the whole proceedings with hard unfeeling eyes.

"Now, Elena, we will settle things between us once and for all." His eyes were dark and unrelenting as they looked at her, and she refused to meet his gaze. "As you've guessed, I now know that you have been forging checks in my name. I find it incredible that you thought you could get away with it for long. My accountant recognized the forgery as soon as the checks came through."

"You could afford it," she brazened it out.

"I don't think that's quite the point," he drawled. "How did you hope to keep me from finding out? Or perhaps," he added shrewdly, "you hoped that by the time I did, it would no longer make any difference to me."

Alex saw from her careless shrug that that was indeed what Elena had hoped, why she had been so determined to come to San Blas and see Marcos. But she hadn't counted on Alex's presence and she had underestimated Marcos.

"So now you have found out," Elena said insolently, "what do you intend to do? Have me arrested? Sophie would just love that, wouldn't she?"

"No, I don't intend to have our family

dragged through another scandal. But Sánchez gave me some very interesting information concerning your financial affairs. Ramón's money is gone. You've been living off Sophie for the past few months, but even Sophie cannot afford to keep up with your expensive tastes. Acapulco, for instance."

"So?" Elena said defiantly.

"So I'll make you a proposition. For certain considerations, I'll provide you with an apartment in Mexico City and settle an annuity on you."

"In return for what?" she asked coldly, but Alex saw the relief that flooded her face.

"You will visit Sophie regularly and never for a moment cause her concern. If you do, your money will be cut off and I will press charges against you. Ten thousand dollars' worth of forgery is quite a felony."

"Then why are you doing this?" she asked bitterly. "Sophie would eventually recover from the shock."

"Because I want you off the *hacienda* and out of my life once and for all! Perhaps I feel that our family did you a great disservice when we took you in as a girl. You grew up regarding the ranch as yours, and it became an obsession with you to become its mistress. Because you were alone, my father petted and pampered you until you believed that anything was yours for the asking—including me. Perhaps later," he added bleakly, "if you had been forced to earn your own living, make a career for yourself, something could have been salvaged. I only hope it isn't too late."

"I don't need your self-righteous nobility, Marcos!" she spat angrily. "Oh, I'll accept your generous offer, and I'll leave you with this—this . . ."

"Elena!" he thundered.

"But at least I have the satisfaction of knowing that I had my revenge! Salvage something from those ashes, if you can!"

His eyes were hard, his lips twisted and mocking, as he looked at her triumphant face. "I hate to disappoint you, Elena. You've burned a good share of the original manuscript, that's true, but I had copies made in Tepic. One is on its way to Boston and another is locked securely in my safe. You took your revenge a day too late! Now get out of my sight while I still remember that I have never hit a woman in my life!"

Alex didn't even see Elena leave. A smile of grim amusement played over her face as she looked at her bandaged hands. All that for nothing! The clink of glasses brought her attention back to Marcos as he poured more brandy and held a glass to her lips. After one swallow, she shook her head.

"Did—did you mean what you said about other copies?"

He took a drink from his own glass before answering. "Yes, but don't think I don't appreciate what you tried to do." Raising his eyes from the swirling liquid, he held her gaze.

"Why did you do it, Alex? When it might have meant the end of your career?"

"I—I just didn't think, I guess."

He opened his lips to speak and then closed them again and ran a hand over his disordered hair. "You left me on the beach," he said abruptly.

The shock of discovering Elena had pushed the earlier episode to the back of her mind, and during the scene that ensued she had been too caught up in the new drama to be embarrassed by Marcos's presence, but now that he had reopened the subject, she felt all the shyness natural to a woman finding herself alone again with the man who now knew every inch of her body. He didn't give her time, however, to dwell on the memory. His voice when he spoke again was far removed from her lover on the beach.

"I spoke to Pieter today—or rather yesterday. He is going to make arrangements for the premiere of *Night Suite* in Boston at the end of the summer."

Her startled eyes met his. "Who—who is going to play it?" she asked breathlessly.

"Why, you, of course!" he stated with a feigned surprise. "Who else?"

Her eyes searched his face for some clue to what he was feeling, but his expression revealed nothing. "What—what did Pieter say?"

"I didn't give him a chance to state his opinion," he answered flatly. "I simply announced that it would be you or no one."

"Why" she asked baldly.

"Why not? Have you changed your mind about pursuing your career?"

How did he want her to answer? "It—it isn't necessary, Marcos . . ." she ventured vaguely.

"And I say it is! I remember a certain bargain between us. Well, I am merely fulfilling my part of it."

"But this is more, so much more!" she whispered desperately.

"You will allow me to know what I consider adequate repayment for . . . services rendered," he said coldly.

Services rendered! Her heart contracted in pain. Was that the name he gave to her surrender? She ought to be flattered that he placed such a high price on her virginity! He was literally putting his professional career in her hands. He had used her, and Symphony Hall was to be her payoff. Then he could consider himself free of further obligation to her. Oh, he was fulfilling his side of their marriage bargain generously, she acknowledged bitterly.

"Well? Why do you hesitate?" His voice interrupted her bitter thoughts. "That's why you married me, isn't it? For your career?" His eyes on her face were hard and searching. Had he shown one sign of tenderness, given one hint that she meant anything to him, she would have thrown herself on his mercy, poured out her love, and begged to stay with him. Instead he turned, gathered up the charred remains of the manuscript, and threw them in the grate.

"Well?" he repeated, his back to her. "Isn't that why you married me?"

"Yes, yes, of course! My career!"

"Then it's settled. You leave day after tomorrow. Pieter will help to arrange the rest of the program, but I think Mozart or Schubert would be a good choice for the first part."

"You—you aren't coming with me?"

"No, there's no need. My work is finished. Yours is just beginning. I know I can trust you to interpret the score as I intended." So easily he dismissed her from his life! "But come," he continued. "It is nearly dawn. We must go to bed."

"Together?" she asked bitterly.

"Why not?" And his smile mocked her.

"You don't consider that I fulfilled my part of the bargain?"

He shrugged, and his eyes were cold. "We only have two days left together, Alex. We may as well make the most of them."

His callousness appalled her, and as he reached out to touch her she shuddered in revulsion. What had he called her? His *woman!* As though she were a mindless body bought for his pleasure. He would love her tonight and the next and then would send her on her way with a careless shrug of his shoulders.

"No, Marcos!"

His eyebrows met above his nose. "You tell me no?"

"Yes!" she said coldly.

"Are you trying to delude me into believing that you did not enjoy what happened between us tonight? You are now my wife, Alex!"

"Your wife? As I remember it, it was your woman—now bought and paid for!"

"But a poor bargain," he drawled, "if you refuse to sleep with me again." His eyes raked her body insolently, and before she could evade him, he grabbed her by the arm. "Come!"

"No! Let me go!"

"I swear you don't mean it. You wanted me tonight as much as I wanted you!"

"I do mean it! Let me go!" His hold was powerful, and in desperation she struggled against him, turning her head and sinking her teeth in his hand on her shoulder.

"*Dios!*" he exclaimed, releasing her. "What you want is not a man but a tame lapdog to lick at your feet!"

Oh, he thought he understood women so well. He knew the response he had aroused in her, but he didn't understand her at all if he thought desire alone would drive her to his bed. She had given herself to him in love— and she wouldn't have that love made cheap.

"No, Marcos," she repeated with quiet dignity. "I realize that it's beyond your comprehension, but what I want is a man who isn't afraid to consider a woman a thinking, feeling equal."

"Afraid? Are you calling me a coward?"

"Yes," she said solemnly, "I think I am. You married me as a protection against the women who pursued you—Elena in particular. Aren't you really afraid that someday some woman will finally break down that barrier of hatred you've built around yourself, and you might just find that you need something more than a means to satisfy your male drives? Then where would you be?" She laughed mirthlessly. "Why, you'd be just as vulnerable as the rest of us. So you relegate our whole sex to the position of playthings, put on earth for your amusement. Well, I for one am not interested in playing anymore."

She saw that her words had had a stunning effect on him. His body had gone rigid, his face frozen like carved granite.

"Is that what you really think of me?" he said bleakly. "After all the time we've spent together, you can believe that? But I guess it's well I know your low opinion of me. Oh, we are a fine pair, aren't we? I use women for my sensual pleasure, and you sell yourself for your career. Now, I would say that we are well matched!"

"Marcos?" Something in his words, his manner, was tearing her apart.

"No, don't say any more! You have said quite enough!" His laugh was hollow. "Are you sure you won't reconsider, Alex? Wouldn't

233

you say that two such amoral creatures deserve each other?"

Dumbly she shook her head. What was he trying to say?

"Never mind!" he said curtly. "We understand each other now, and at least you have the satisfaction of knowing that you won't have to endure my presence much longer."

Just for a moment his hand reached out to her, but then it dropped to his side and without another word he turned on his heel and strode from the room. Wordlessly Alex followed, her eyes filled with tears of pain and regret.

Well, she had done it. He would never forgive her. She had made the break, if not cleanly at least completely. But wasn't that better than living in the hopeless position of loving him, living with him occasionally, but knowing that she would never mean anything to him? At least now she could try to forget him and begin the task of putting her life back together.

Yes, it was over, she thought desolately— her stay, her marriage, her hope for happiness—her own personal Mexican rhapsody.

Chapter Eleven

Alex leaned her head against the hard back of the leather easy chair and looked around the dressing room. The events of the past four months might never have taken place. The room was just as she had seen it last, only now a bouquet of red roses graced the table—a tribute from Pieter—and the pictures staring out at her from the folded newspaper brought memories too bittersweet to bear: *Marcos Rivera. Alexandra Stephanos.*

The photograph of Marcos was an old one, obviously pulled from Pieter's files. It showed him as she remembered him from her teenage years, but it bore no resemblance to the man she had come to know and love, who had stood silent and grim on the dilapidated steps of *Casa de Rivera* as Tomás drove the car away from the house.

The past two months had helped to deaden the pain somewhat, and it helped also that she had soon begun working on the material for the concert. The introduction of *Night*

Suite had been scheduled for late August, and once her hands had healed, she drove herself, practicing ten and twelve hours a day. She refused to talk with Pieter about her experiences in San Blas, but his shrewd eyes had seen all that she would have concealed, and after the first few days he stopped asking her painful questions.

With a sigh Alex stood and smoothed down the soft blue crêpe of her dress. She had flatly refused to wear black, though she often felt as though she were in mourning, and the graceful folds of the fabric falling from the high waist helped to conceal the weight she had lost in the past weeks. Her hair was once again pulled back into a tight chignon, but she had softened the effect with curls over her ears. She grimaced at her pale self in the mirror and stopped to smooth on more blusher and freshen her lipstick.

"You are nervous, little one?" said a voice behind her, and she smiled at Pieter's reflection.

"I didn't hear you come in, Pieter. Is the house nearly in?"

"Another ten, fifteen minutes, perhaps," he shrugged.

"Did—did you ever hear from Marcos?" she asked casually, all her attention seemingly fixed on smoothing her already perfect hair.

"I told you he called me after I sent him the advance publicity pictures and articles," he answered vaguely, flipping out his tails and perching like a bird on the edge of a straight chair. "Quit fussing with your hair, Alexandra," he added testily. "I am not going to ask you any embarrassing questions. You are a woman now, not the green girl I sent to Mexico. And I have every confidence that you are quite capable of sorting out your own life without the help of a romantic old man."

A rueful smile lit Alex's eyes and for a moment dispelled the shadows that had lingered there so long. "I wish I had the same confidence, Pieter."

"All will come right, Alexandra. You will see."

"I saw yesterday's paper. Did—did you have to publicize the fact that I'm Marcos's wife?" she asked gruffly, straightening the buttons on her full sleeves.

"I was only following his instructions, my dear. Better even than fine music, the world loves a romance. And what could be more romantic than that the wife of the esteemed Marcos Rivera perform his first masterpiece when he is unable to do so himself?"

"It *is* a masterpiece, isn't it?" she asked, lifting anxious eyes to his. "I—I've loved it from the first moment I played it."

"As you love the man himself, eh?"

"Pieter, please!"

"All right, all right. I won't upset you now, but I will tell you that it is your love that makes the playing transcendent. I have never heard you better, my dear."

"Oh, I hope so!"

"And I think it was a wise choice to use the *Mexican Rhapsody* as the encore. It will bring even the critics to their feet."

The knock on the door of the dressing room signaled the ten-minute warning.

"But there, I must go," Pieter said, puffing to his feet. "You have them standing in the aisles tonight." He paused to pat her cheek with his plump hand. "Do Nikolas and me proud tonight, little one."

"And Marcos," she added softly.

"And Marcos."

Alex's hands flew firmly and surely over the keys as she unfolded the magic of *Night Suite*. The weeks of intensive practice had given her touch even greater strength and dexterity, and tonight her emotions ran so near to the surface of her calm façade. The great crowd-filled hall faded from her consciousness. Once again she was back in San Blas, back in the music room, and she felt Marcos's presence, his strength, his genius, reaching out to her, strengthening her, pushing her on to greater and greater heights. All her love for him poured out of her and into his music. Forgotten was the pain and humiliation she had suffered. All she remembered were the good times—their shared love of music, the evenings spent together in mutual pleasure and harmony, the rapture she had found in his arms.

The third movement—*The Lovers*—held new meaning for her. The last—*The Dawn*—echoed her uncertainty in the future. The last poignant moments built to the runs and final chords, and all her hopes and fears were infused into the music. The silence as she finished was absolute. Then came the applause, the cries of "Bravo!" that echoed through the hall. Slowly Alex lost her inner vision and came back to reality, but for once the thundering ovation, the acclaim of the audience, meant everything to her—not for herself but for Marcos. Tonight would elevate him as a composer to rank with the geniuses of modern music.

For a moment her eyes blurred with tears as she rose from her seat and faced the crowd, her heart filled with joyous thanksgiving as she swept them a deep curtsy. Oh, if only Marcos were here to see this reception of his work!

Again and again she bowed, until suddenly a slight movement in the wings caught her attention. There stood Pieter, and beside him a beloved, familiar figure in white tie and tails. Marcos! Of their own volition her hands went out to him, and slowly he came across the stage to join her. Only when he was close enough for her to see the gleam of pride in his deep, jade-green eyes did she believe that the fabric of her dreams had become substance.

He took her hands in his and pressed his lips into each palm. Together they turned to their public and acknowledged the tumultuous applause that filled the hall.

"Will you give them an encore?" he asked as the moments passed.

"Yes."

The crowd quieted as he led her to the piano and then retreated to the wings.

"Ladies and gentlemen," she said into the silence, "another new work by Marcos Rivera —*Mexican Rhapsody*."

Marcos is here! her heart sang, and she played with all the pride and love of country that she knew he had invested in the work. The audience's response at the conclusion was all and more than she could have hoped for, and once again Marcos joined her onstage as the audience rose to its feet. Together they took their bows, and in a daze Alex allowed him to lead her into the wings and then back onstage again—a third, a fourth, a fifth time. At last Marcos signaled the stage manager, and the houselights were brought up, the lights on stage dimmed.

"Thank you, Alex," Marcos said soberly. "I don't think even I could have played my music so well."

"Little one!" Pieter's voice boomed in her ear, his arms enfolded her, and she was crushed against his chest, his cheek against hers—and Alex could feel the tears that streamed down his face. "You were magnificent, my dear! Brilliant! As of course I knew you would be!"

"Oh, Pieter!" Alex whispered. "He came."

"Yes, my darling. He came."

She pulled away and looked into his face. "You knew he was going to be here!"

"Not until a week ago."

"Why didn't you tell me?"

"Even if he had not asked that I didn't, I wouldn't have done. It was better that you did not know."

"Where is he?" She looked around as people began milling onto the backstage area. She couldn't see him anywhere. "He's gone!" A sense of overwhelming loss made her weak, and she clutched at Pieter's sleeve.

"Come. I will take you to your dressing room." Arm around her waist, he helped her down the stairs.

"He's gone!" she cried as Pieter closed the door behind them.

"You will see him again later, at the reception. Now rest for a while. I'll see that you are not disturbed until it is time to leave."

Wearily Alex sank down in the chair. Marcos had come and then he had gone again, before she had had a chance to talk to him. He knew now, of course, about her deception—who she really was. Did he feel that she had made a fool of him? Oh, how he must hate her!

Alex didn't see him again until an hour later at the reception Pieter had arranged at the Parker House, and a great sea of people separated them. It was impossible to get near him, and Alex forced herself to return the greetings from fellow musicians, friends, and critics. She smiled, spoke, turned, smiled, spoke—scarcely knowing what she was saying. Yes, Pieter had arranged a record contract for *Night Suite*. No, after New York and San Francisco, she wasn't sure where she would perform next. Her heart contracted painfully. No, they weren't sure if Marcos would be able to accompany her on the tour. No, she really couldn't say what his plans were next. Why didn't they ask him themselves?

On and on the questions, answers, smiles went, and not until well after midnight did the crowd begin to thin. Alex felt the weariness of complete emotional exhaustion. Desperately she longed to escape.

Suddenly, she felt the touch on her arm. Only one man had ever been able to make her nerves quiver, her senses hum, at a single touch. Slowly she turned and looked straight into Marcos's eyes.

"You're ready to collapse," he said gently. "Come. Pieter knows I am taking you away now."

Mechanically she moved with him through the crowd, his supporting arm around her waist. One last embrace from Pieter, a flurry of farewells, a round of applause from their well-wishers—and Marcos whisked her out the door and into the elevator.

They were alone. For weeks she had longed to see him again, but now that he was here, she was so afraid. All those bitter words they had spoken rose to haunt her. Had he come to ask for a divorce? In his presence she was fast losing the pride that had sustained her through the last terrible weeks. She was reaching the point that, if necessary, she would beg him, plead with him, to take her back—on any terms!

Sick at heart, she leaned against the back wall and deliberately kept her head averted from Marcos beside her, focusing her attention on the lighted floor numbers above the door. Five, six, seven, eight . . . Where were they going? The elevator was moving up, not down! She turned startled eyes to Marcos, and he answered her unspoken question.

"We're going up to my room," he said tersely. "I promised Pieter that I would do nothing to upset you this evening, but now we must talk!"

"Please, Marcos," she pleaded, dreading the thought that this was the end, "not tonight. I—I couldn't stand to quarrel with you now."

"Who says we're going to quarrel?" His lips set in a tight, straight line. "Alex, I refuse to live through another day with our future unresolved."

What did he mean? Alex wondered wildly.

As the elevator doors slid silently open he

took her hand and pulled it through his arm. It was still there—the electricity of his touch.

Wordlessly he led her down the thick, plush carpet to his room and ushered her inside. "Sit down, please," he said curtly and after a glance at her pale face added, "Will you have a little brandy?"

Dumbly she nodded as her eyes took in the luxurious intimacy of the room and came to rest on the large double bed.

"Relax!" he drawled as he crossed to the built-in bar. "I haven't brought you here to attack you!"

She had thought that he was hostile, angry with her, but as he poured the brandy into the glasses she saw that his hand was shaking. He was just as tense as she!

"Why have you brought me here?" she asked carefully as she took a sustaining sip from the glass he pressed into her hand.

"We've got to talk," he repeated doggedly.

"And end up quarreling again," she murmured bitterly.

His voice was bleak as he replied, "Our talks didn't always end in quarrels, if you'll remember."

"No," she whispered softly, her eyes dark with memory. "No, they didn't. So—so what do you want to discuss?"

"You don't think Alexandra Stephanos needs a bit of explaining?" he asked quietly.

He spoke so gently, so mildly. Where was

the anger, the disgust, she had steeled herself to accept as her just punishment? His gaze was intent and searching, but his eyes held a lurking warmth that gave her fresh courage, new hope.

"Marcos," she said in a rush before the courage could desert her, "I—I'm sorry, so sorry—about deceiving you, I mean. I want you to believe that when I came to San Blas using my real name instead of my professional name, I didn't come to trick you in some way or try to make a fool of you. I—I just wanted to escape—my past, my old self. And suddenly I was caught up in my own deception. I didn't want to be Alexandra Stephanos anymore, and I didn't want you to find out the truth. . . . Oh, I don't know how to make you understand!" She knew her words were practically incoherent, but she felt as though a terrible burden had been lifted from her, and her eyes pleaded with Marcos for understanding.

"But a *nightclub*, Alex?"

"You made me angry," she said woefully, hanging her head in shame.

"I can see I will have to be very careful in the future!"

Something in the tone of his voice brought her head up with a snap. His one eyebrow was cocked and the corner of his mouth twitched. He was laughing!

"Marcos?" she questioned, bewildered.

"Alex, *mi amor,*" he murmured. "None of those terrible suspicions you mention ever crossed my mind. I was too relieved, too grateful! You can't begin to know how thankful I was when I learned the truth!"

Her mouth opened in a silent gasp, and she stared at him with wide, incredulous eyes. "Thankful?"

"Yes, thankful!" The humor left his face, and he turned on the couch, the better to see her changing expressions. "Why do you think I am here tonight, Alex?" he asked softly.

"B-because of the concert? . . ." she began hesitantly.

"No! I came to repeat a question I have asked you before: Why did you marry me, Alex?"

That was not at all what she had expected, and she was taken aback. "I—I don't understand. Why do you care?"

"Because, my little liar, Alex Stephens might be able to convince me that she married me to further her career, but for Alexandra Stephanos to marry for such a reason is absurd, inconceivable. She already had a brilliant career waiting for her if she chose to pursue it. So I repeat: Why did you marry me?"

"Ohhh," Alex breathed as enlightenment dawned. A blush rose in her face and then faded, leaving her paler than before. "Why— why do you think I married you, then?" she countered nervously.

"That's what I have come nearly four thousand miles to hear you tell me!"

"And—and does the answer matter to you?" she asked, hope rising in her heart.

"It makes all the difference between heaven and hell!"

"I know a little about outer darkness myself, Marcos," she said soberly. "You sent me away!"

He gathered her hands in his own and held them against his chest. "Don't you see, my darling? I had to! I had come to love you with all my heart, but I didn't know how you felt about me. I thought that by offering to fulfill my part of the bargain I would force you to choose between a real marriage and the kind of career I had promised you. You see, I had such hopes! I had overheard you talking with Elena. You told her that you loved me, but I didn't know if what you said was true or part of our pretense, so I watched and waited." His voice grew husky. "I was determined to make love to you, to show you what our marriage could offer."

Desperately she wanted to believe him, but she couldn't yet. "But you didn't want a wife," she whispered brokenly. "Part-time wife. That was what you said. No little woman around the house—"

He placed his fingers against her lips. "*Querida,* at that moment I would have said anything to have won you! If freedom was what you wanted, freedom you would have."

"You—you loved me then?"

A frown gathered on his face. "I honestly don't know, my darling. I was still hurt, disillusioned, distrustful of women. All I knew was that when I announced that we were married, more than anything in this world I wanted it to be true. No woman had ever affected me as you did, and I was angry—with you, with myself—that you had become such a necessary part of my life. I had wanted you for weeks, and I believed that the wanting was enough. But by our wedding night—which was no wedding night—I had to face the fact that sometime, somehow, the wanting had become loving. And when we made love," he murmured huskily, "I knew that you were my only hope of heaven on this earth!"

His words were quietly spoken, but their soft intensity devastated her, and she was stricken with remorse. "Oh, Marcos, all those terrible things I said to you that night!" she wailed.

"They hurt, my love. I have been able to think of nothing else for two months! What happened that night to make you turn on me like that?"

"You were going to send me away," she replied simply. "In the beginning you had asked me what made me different from any other woman, and I didn't know. I only knew that I loved you, but I didn't think my love counted for anything with you. I was so frightened and hurt!"

He flinched at the pain in her words. "And when I offered you your career, you accepted, and I thought I had lost you forever. It wasn't until I received Pieter's letter telling me that no less a personage than Alexandra Stephanos—alias Alex Stephens, alias Mrs. Marcos Rivera—was going to perform my work that I found new hope, and I knew I had to see you, change your opinion of me—"

"Oh, Marcos! There's nothing to change! I think I must have loved you since the first time I saw you in London!"

"And I have only the vague memory of a serious, skinny schoolgirl." He sighed regretfully. "Who would have thought then that tonight she would be the toast of the music world?"

"Marcos!" she cried as the thought struck her. "We haven't even talked about the concert!"

His eyes were suddenly filled with light and laughter. "My darling, don't you think we've done enough talking for one night? We've our whole lives to talk about our work together. We might, for example, think of your concert tour as a honeymoon. Hmmm? But right now," he added softly, "it is very late, and I am very anxious to take my beautiful wife to bed!"

He pulled her unresisting into his arms. Hungrily they shared the first kiss of their acknowledged love. All restraint was gone. Instant passion surged between them. His one hand sought her breast through the soft crêpe of her gown, and then with a moan of impatience his other found the zipper at the nape of her neck.

"You are overdressed," he murmured against her lips. "I far prefer your bikini." And she felt a thrill of anticipation as his fingers slid down her spine and the offending garment dropped to the floor.

Her own hands were not idle. She slipped two fingers into the opening in his shirt and pulled gently at the curling hair on his chest. He shivered with pleasure and turned his face against her neck, drawing little circles with his tongue until she moaned with desire.

"You taste sweet tonight." He gently nibbled at her shoulder.

"No salt from the sea," she whispered foolishly.

"No, just the taste—of you! A gourmet's delight!"

Heavenly nonsense!

"Oh, Marcos! I love you so much!" She slipped her arms beneath his coat to press herself tightly against him. Impatiently he shrugged out of it, but as his hands moved to his white tie she stopped him. "No, let me!"

There was delicious pleasure in the small intimacy as she slowly and deliberately tugged at one end of the formal bow tie and then pulled it from under his collar. As she began on the buttons of his shirt she felt his hands in her hair, removing the pins that held her chignon in place. One by one the pins dropped to the floor until her hair cascaded down over her bare shoulders.

As she struggled with the cummerbund around his waist he covered her hands with his and smiled down into her face. "You are as impatient as I, my love. We are going to have to see that you have more practice, but for now I cannot wait any longer!"

Quickly he removed the remainder of his clothing and then hers. Lifting her high against his heart, he laid her gently on the bed. For just a moment his eyes devoured her, and then, with the sureness and precision of a true virtuoso, Marcos once again began his love theme.

Alex's head began to swim as he raised her to greater and greater heights of pleasure, and his words of adoration, the touch of his hands on her body, the feel of his lips on hers, were sweeter than any music.

His body moved to lie over hers. Once again she knew the ecstatic delight of his possession, and she was sure—quite sure—that she heard a rhapsody singing in her veins—the melody sweet and lilting and tender, the ornamentation exquisite, the counterpoint strong and deep with passion. Together they soared to a crescendo that carried them into bliss.

For long moments Alex pulsated along on wave after wave of pleasure, until at last she buried her face against Marcos's chest and gave a deep sigh of contentment.

Yes, she thought when she could think at all, a rhapsody!

If you enjoyed this book...

...you will enjoy a Special Edition Book Club membership even more.

It will bring you each new title, as soon as it is published every month, delivered right to your door.

15-Day Free Trial Offer

We will send you 6 new Silhouette Special Editions to keep for 15 days absolutely free! If you decide not to keep them, send them back to us, you pay nothing. But if you enjoy them as much as we think you will, keep them and pay the invoice enclosed with your trial shipment. You will then automatically become a member of the Special Edition Book Club and receive 6 more romances every month. There is no minimum number of books to buy and you can cancel at any time.

Silhouette Special Edition

Coming Next Month

Silver Mist by Sondra Stanford

Laurel Patterson ran away with her sister and niece to a
small town in Texas to escape from a disastrous love
affair. To finally free her mind from the painful
memories, Laurel concentrates all her energy on setting
up the child-care center she and her sister are starting.
Then Stephen Tanner, a local rancher, enters her world
and proceeds to win over her sister and niece. Laurel
slowly and unwillingly succumbs to his charms and
irresistible manner. But now that Laurel has adjusted to
the challenge of a new life and a new business, the
hardest challenge of all is adjusting to a new man.

Texas Rose by Katharine Thiels

Alexis Kellogg's big breakthrough as a reporter brought
her back to the town she had left in scandal—and into the
arms of the man who drove her away. Cade Morse was one
of the richest men in Texas and Alexis' job was to discover
what drove him to the top. Was her destiny in his arms
. . . or in the truth she was sent to unearth, the article she
was compelled to write?

Never Give Your Heart by Tracy Sinclair

Gillian North was thrilled to land the Bliss Cosmetics
account, but not with Bliss owner, Roman Barclay, who
was determined to make Gillian part of the deal.

Then, quickly, things changed between them, and Gillian
began to dream of a shared future. But the dream was
shattered when Roman showed, unmistakably,
just what she was to him: a prize
possession, expensively bought.

She knew her heart was lost; could she salvage her pride?

Coming Next Month

Keys To Daniel's House by Carole Halston

Sydney Cullen had no use for men. All her energies went into her family and her career. The accusation that her looks were behind her success stung, and she grasped the chance to disprove the statement.

How could she have known that in using Daniel Bates to prove her point she would prove only that, no matter how hard she tried, she could never escape her own needs, her own passions?

All Our Tomorrows by Mary Lynn Baxter

Ex-tennis star Brooke Lawson's brother insists she recover from her crippling car accident at his home in Hawaii. Faced with the possible end to her career, Brooke struggles to regain her confidence and physical strength amidst her tormenting attraction to entrepreneur, Ashley Graham. Ashley, a hard-driving and virile man, arranges a marriage with her which she must accept to learn the depth of her passion for him. But can she continue a forced commitment to a man who demands all of her?

Love Is Surrender by Carolyn Thornton

Jennifer Waring, an attractive, young journalist, heartbroken over her divorce, felt like she belonged to another era as she drove down the treelined drive to the Esplanade plantation. She had been hired to publicize Esplanade and its owner, Ham Bertout. Ham relights the flame of desire within Jennifer, as she does in him. It is Jennifer's desire to do what is right and to be certain her love for her ex-husband is over that nearly destroys their new found love.

MORE ROMANCE FOR
A SPECIAL WAY TO RELAX

_____ #1	TERMS OF SURRENDER Janet Dailey	$1.95
_____ #2	INTIMATE STRANGERS Brooke Hastings	$1.95
_____ #3	MEXICAN RHAPSODY Diana Dixon	$1.95
_____ #4	VALAQUEZ BRIDE Donna Vitek	$1.95
_____ #5	PARADISE POSTPONED Jane Converse	$1.95
_____ #6	SEARCH FOR A NEW DAWN Billie Douglass	$1.95

SILHOUETTE SPECIAL EDITION, Department SE/2
1230 Avenue of the Americas
New York, NY 10020

Please send me the books I have checked above. I am enclosing $_____
(please add 50¢ to cover postage and handling. NYS and NYC residents
please add appropriate sales tax). Send check or money order—no cash or
C.O.D.'s please. Allow six weeks for delivery.

NAME _____

ADDRESS _____

CITY _____ STATE/ZIP _____